Herbert J. Spiro,

editor of this volume, is Professor of Political Science at the University of Penn-
sylvania and former chairman of the
Asian and African Studies Program of
Amherst, Mt. Holyoke, and Smith Colleges and the University of Massachusetts. He has traveled widely in Africa
on Guggenheim, Fulbright, and Social
Science Research fellowships; is a Fellow
of the African Studies Association; has
lectured on U.S. Policy toward Africa
under the auspices of the USIA in
Germany; and has given courses on
African politics at Harvard, the University of Chicago, Stanford, and Princeton.
Among his other publications are *Government by Constitution* (1959), *Politics
in Africa* (1962), *Africa: The Primacy of
Politics* (1966), and *World Politics: The
Global System* (1966).

Patterns
of
African Development

Patterns
of
African Development
Five Comparisons

edited by
HERBERT J. SPIRO

Prentice-Hall, Inc. *Englewood Cliffs, N.J.*

Preface

Most writers on African politics have been Western scholars who too often base their work upon one of two erroneous assumptions: either that the pattern of African development is wholly unique, or that the new African "peanut republics" will simply repeat patterns established earlier by Latin American "banana republics." A few Africans have also written about the politics of their continent, but they have generally been politicians, not scholars.

This book was written by one African and four American political scientists who have avoided the assumptions both of total uniqueness and of eternal repetition. Instead of drawing misleading analogies from apparently similar patterns in other areas and earlier eras of state-building, nationalism, modernization, and political philosophizing, we have sought to observe the rules of valid analogy. It is, of course, up to the reader to judge our success.

The book literally "grew" out of papers originally prepared for the Eighth Annual Meeting of the African Studies Association, held in Philadelphia in October, 1965. The growth was, from the editor's point of view, wholly nonmalignant, and I wish to thank my colleagues and the editors of Spectrum Books at Prentice-Hall for their patience and their punctuality.

H.J.S.

Contents

II

III

IV

Borrowed Theory
and Original Practice
in African Politics – *Ali A. Mazrui,* 91

V

Repetition or Innovation? – *Herbert J. Spiro,* 125

Patterns
of
African Development

Introduction

Herbert J. Spiro

I – Five *"Developing Areas"*

Recent literature on Africa has generally been written and received as part of the growing body of information and analysis of the so-called *developing areas*. Before this term came into general usage, both popular and academic, such phrases as *underdeveloped countries* and *non-Western areas* enjoyed wide currency. However, emphasis upon *under*development carried with it the negative imputation of backwardness and may even have been regarded as somehow impolite, by both those who made it and those to whose countries it was applied. The same seemed true of the *non*-Western label, which, moreover, was inaccurate when applied to most Latin American countries. *Development,* on the other hand, was deliberately intended by some initiators of the concept of developing areas to "accentuate the positive." At the same time, this phrase also pointed to regional or areal interdependence among states which, in many cases, became states under international law only after creation of the vocabulary of the study of the developing areas.

Along with the literature on the developing areas, and after the usual time lag, the body of criticism of this literature has also been growing. The focus of these critiques naturally varies a good deal, but most of them seem to accept rather *un*critically the concept of developing areas and its applicability to the five regions usually described by it: South Asia, Southeast Asia, the Middle East, Latin America, and Africa. Both the original and the critical writings show an awareness, to varying degrees, that each of these regions has its own distinctive features. Scholars argue about the relative importance of the major differences among the areas and about

1

the causes and likely consequences of these differences. But they generally agree that all are most usefully described and analyzed as developing areas or, to put it more concretely, that the focus of attention should be upon development—its rate, scope, effectiveness, direction, and other aspects.

This scholarly consensus raises several practical questions for politicians and students of politics in general, and in particular for students of politics in these regions:

First: Do the concepts *development* and *developing areas* provide a basis for useful classification? In other words, can we advance our understanding by grouping countries (or other political systems) in regions, and by placing them along a spectrum that runs from the underdeveloped through the developing to the developed and perhaps on to the overdeveloped?

Second: If the first question is answered affirmatively, just what is it that is developing? Is it the economy, the society, the culture, political institutions or procedures or participation, or something else? And if several or all of these are engaged in the process of development, what are the patterns of relations among them?

Third: How much can we learn from one developing area about another, for example, from the experience of Latin America or Southeast Asia for the generally later development of Black Africa? Will this help us, as insiders trying to develop our own countries, or as outsiders trying to analyze the behavior of—and perhaps to help—the insiders.

Or does the suggestion of likeness, implied by the common application to all these areas of the label *developing,* already answer the third question? Will what happened in one area, after allowance has been made for obvious differences, have to be repeated in the others? Since Africa is a developing area, will its major problems and main trends have to follow the patterns of experience of the four other areas whose development began earlier, and also the still earlier experience of the United States of America, which some regard as the first and most successful case of modern development?

II – Four Perspectives

All of these questions were boiled down into one, which I addressed to my distinguished colleagues on the Political Science Panel at the Eighth Annual Meeting of the African Studies Association: "Africa and Other Developing Areas: Repetition or Innovation?" They are all political scientists, but their backgrounds and the reasons for their interest in African affairs are rather diverse.

Carl J. Friedrich has been concerned with the universals of politics, in the true sense of those words. I therefore asked Professor Friedrich to consider critically the validity of singling out development as a qualitatively novel or different aspect of politics.

Ibrahim Abu-Lughod, as a student of Egyptian nationalism and of international relations, enjoys an especially advantageous perspective from which to compare nationalism in Black Africa with the domestic and international manifestations of older forms of nationalism in another part of that continent, in other Islamic countries outside Africa, and in other developing and developed areas.

Claude E. Welch, Jr., belongs to the youngest generation of political scientists with a special interest in Africa. He is well qualified to approach answers to our central question by comparing the processes of modernization in Japan and Africa and the role of governments in modernizing. He thereby broadens the total perspective of this book beyond the usual comparisons among developing areas—one of Mr. Abu-Lughod's tasks—and beyond the "conventional" comparisons between them and the older national states of Europe—undertaken by Mr. Friedrich—to include the most dramatic, and most widely studied, non-western instance of deliberate self-modernization.

Ali A. Mazrui, himself an African, deals with the kind of "gutty" philosophical questions that insiders and participants are much better qualified to answer than outside observers. I remember a conversation I had in 1960 with a prominent leader of Africans in Southern Rhodesia, who was subsequently jailed for political reasons. Unlike most of his colleagues at the time, this politician rather deprecated the helpfulness of liberal white Rhodesians to his cause. "After all, white people cannot understand what we feel in our black chests," he told me, with a smile, and pounding his black chest. There was wisdom in that remark, and I believe that Professor Mazrui—not known to pound his chest, though at least as eloquent as Mr. Leopold Takawira of Zimbabwe—is better qualified than any white scholar to discuss "Borrowed Theory and Original Practice in African Politics," precisely because his mastery of the literature and methods of our discipline is complemented by the kind of existential empathy which only a black African can feel for his fellows.

III – Three Questions

It may be useful in this Introduction to attempt preliminary answers to my three prior questions about the concept of development.

First: Does *development* provide a basis for useful classification?

If, by *development,* we mean growth of some sort, then we should be able to agree upon the occurrence of development in the five areas concerned, and certainly in Black Africa. Development in this sense has occurred previously in other regions and countries, including, in reverse chronological order, Russia, Japan, and the United States of America. Of course, development is still going on in these mature, highly developed countries, but obviously from a much more advanced base line than, say, in Portugal, Vietnam, and Brazil. This suggests that development may be viewed from two different aspects that should be—but rarely are—clearly distinguished: level of development, and process of developing. For example, Sweden is obviously more developed than Kenya, but it seems almost equally evident that there is today more development going on—partly because there is more to be developed—in Kenya than in Sweden. Failure to make this distinction between level and process is often due to lack of clarity about the subjects and objects of development, our second question.

There are two related errors that often flow from use of an unrefined notion of development for purposes of classification and comparison. One of these errors, resulting largely from historical nearsightedness, consists of assuming or asserting the historical uniqueness of contemporary development in these five areas, as though development analogous to the contemporary level or process, in at least some of its aspects, has never occurred anywhere else. This assumption is related to the second error, namely, the belief that the study of the developing areas today calls for methods quite different from those used in the study of, say, the development of England in the Industrial Revolution or of Germany in the nineteenth century both before and after national unification. Partly on the basis of this belief whole new professional "cadres" have been trained to specialize in the study of contemporary developing areas. Their training has sometimes left these new specialists with inadequate familiarity with the history of countries which passed through possibly analogous levels or processes of development in earlier eras. Overspecialization has resulted, and intellectual exchange between students of different historical periods of development, in different areas of the world, has thus been discouraged.

Second: Just what is it that is developing?

There is little clarity about the subjects and objects of development. To the extent that any scholarly agreement can be discerned, it is confined to the importance—for some even the primacy—of development of the economy, partly, perhaps, because this can apparently be quantified and therefore measured most easily. Gross national product either grows or it does not grow. When it is growing, this can be seen, felt, heard, and sometimes smelled and tasted. Tons of concrete and steel and oil, miles of road and numbers of homes constructed, along with social services provided and changes in consumption patterns can be measured more easily than social, cultural, and political growth.

This easier accessibility of economic data has led many scholars —and probably more policy-makers—to jump to the conclusion that economic development occurs before development in the other spheres and must therefore be the cause, or at least a precondition, of noneconomic development. Now, even if economic development could be segregated, for purely analytical purposes, from development in the social, cultural, and political spheres, the reverse sequence of events seems to be closer to the truth; i.e., political development takes place before economic, social, and cultural development, and the development of politics can be looked upon as a condition of other, more substantive types of development.[1] However, these different aspects of the life of men in communities— the political, economic, social, and cultural—can not be sharply segregated from one another because they are in fact only aspects of a whole process. For analytical purposes we can, at best, recognize certain time lags or discontinuities.

It is also true that we can detect among leaders of developing countries differences of both emphasis and desired sequence of achievement. It may be a peculiarity of Black Africa that most of its leaders generally place stronger emphasis upon political than upon economic development and that many of them have professed a belief in and a commitment to the primacy of politics. To understand the relative weight accorded to political, economic, social, cultural, and other forms of development in various areas we need clearer criteria of development than we now have. For example,

[1] See my article "The Primacy of Political Development" in *Africa: The Primacy of Politics*, H. J. Spiro, ed. (New York: Random House, Inc. 1966), pp. 150-69.

does political development consist of approaching Western political practices, building copies of Western political institutions, and joining the Western camp in international politics? Or of emulating Communist models? Or does political development consist of an increase in political participation, the generation of a greater volume of issues for politics, the forging and popularizing of new goals? Which is a better index of political development: the stability and consensus of indifference and stagnation, or the fluidity and dissensus of ferment and of the recognition of new possibilities for political action? Each of these finds its advocates as an index of political development.

Moreover, despite the apparently easy measurability of economic development, similar disagreements persist even among its students. What is the criterion here: gross national product, per capita annual income, government expenditures as a fraction of GNP? the ratio between private and public expenditures, between the industrial and the agricultural sectors, or between the modern and the subsistence economies? distribution of incomes, or the proportion of children in school, or average calorie intake, or the radio and television sets and automobiles per thousand people? Or is it the rates of growth in all these various indices? Each of these, and various combinations of them, has its advocates among students of economic development. These difficulties point to the much greater difficulty of identifying not only the subjects and objects of development but also its causes, conditions, and motives.

Third: How much can one learn from one developing area about another?

We can always gain new insights into the universals of politics and other activities from valid comparisons between comparable human responses to problems arising out of the universals of the human condition. If development is such a universal, which occurs in different eras and areas in a variety of sequences and in response to a variety of conditions, then we can learn from "development comparisons" so long as we allow for the variations. People in the developing areas themselves should be able to draw lessons, at the least from the experience of earlier developers with the handling of specific problems, e.g., in the fields of transportation, production, distribution, and the like. The extraction of the same mineral raises pretty much the same purely technical problems whether in Iran, Nigeria, Venezuela, Chile, or Zambia. But once we try to gauge the impact of an oil field or a copper mining complex on the culture and society, on the economy and politics of rather different countries, the limits of the comparison become apparent. For the knowledge of the older experience itself becomes a factor in the new situation which further complicates the drawing of valid analogies. This applies regardless of the objective accuracy of the knowledge involved. For instance, the developers of hydroelectric power in Ghana may have had a true or a distorted picture of the experience with similar problems of their forerunners in Rhodesia and elsewhere, but their awareness of this previous experience in itself made their own experience different.

IV – *Analogies and Consciousness*

This complicating factor in analogies[2] has special importance for analogies between political situations, in view of the crucial role of consciousness for politics in general, and in particular for the politics of the developing areas. Ultimately, development results from the heightened consciousness of somebody, whether it is a colonial administration, imperialist businessmen, an indigenous elite, or the native masses. Whether development occurs primarily in the economy, the society, the culture, or the polity, or in all of these, in whatever combination, it occurs because there are some people somewhere whose awareness of the possibilities of change has grown and who act on the basis of that awareness. Their awareness may rest on many grave misconceptions, and their actions may produce the very opposite of their intentions, but it is this growth of awareness, converted into the stuff of politics, that stimulates development.

The processes that generate, within and among communities, growth of awareness of the possibilities of change and that result in action upon the real conditions of life in order to produce desired changes—these processes are the core of politics. They go on in all communities, regardless of their level, period, or stage of development. They are performed in a variety of political styles, which can be compared systematically.[3] These are the universals of politics; they are not unique in the developing areas. The call for new methods with which to study the politics of the developing areas was

[2] For a discussion of the rules of valid analogies see my *World Politics: The Global System* (Homewood, Ill.: The Dorsey Press, 1966), pp. 26-35.
[3] See my "Comparative Politics: A Comprehensive Approach," *American Political Science Review*, LVI (Sept. 1962), 577-95.

therefore out of order, unless it was intended to bring about improvements in the methods applied to the study of all politics. At the same time, the feasibility of making analogies between "rock-bottom" political processes, no matter where or when they are occurring, does not imply validity for any and all analogies between different developing countries. For instance, the development problems of the white settlers in North America in the 1780s were quite different from the development problems of black Nigeria in the 1960s. The international problems of the white settlers in North America cannot be studied by analogy to the international problems of the white settlers in Southern Rhodesia in the 1960s, in the age of decolonization and the United Nations—in spite of the profoundly mistaken analogy to 1776 on which the Rhodesians based their Unilateral Declaration of Independence in 1965. The Burmese, who are not heirs to the traditions of Greek dialectical logic or Judaeo-Christian individualism, are likely to respond to problems of economic development differently from their white, Western economic advisers. We often make misplaced analogies between two situations simply because the actors in them erroneously view them as analogous; e.g., when Asian leaders consider their development problems by analogy to those of the Soviet Union in the 1920s, or when Latin American leaders consider theirs by analogy to those of the United States in the 1860s. Analogies are valid only to the extent that there is a similarity in the relations among the components of two different situations. No such relational similarity exists in the cases just cited, even though there may appear to be some substantive resemblance between the problems faced—to move from the sublime to the ridiculous—by a Thomas Jefferson and an Ian Smith. Sometimes leaders of developing countries try to solve their own problems by learning from the nonanalogous and therefore irrelevant experience of others. This frequently has disastrous results, especially if their policies are based upon a rigidly ideological commitment to the validity of the false analogy.

I consider it one of the principal and yet most difficult tasks of political science to create and apply criteria of valid analogizing. This is the task faced by the authors of following chapters: to determine whether analogies among the various developing areas are valid, whether Africans have in fact acted on the basis of such analogies, and whether the resulting pattern of development in Africa evinces repetition or innovation.

I

Some Reflections on Constitutionalism
for Emergent Political Orders

Carl J. Friedrich

Government in the so-called developing countries—countries, that is, which have only recently joined the Western national communities in a process of rapid economic development—is vital to their future. The earlier notion, implied in the thought patterns associated with the now all-but-forgotten idea of a "white man's burden," that the solution lay in establishing Western democracy in these new countries, has been undermined by experience. In country after country serious difficulties have been encountered in making such Western schemes work. Nor is this really surprising, considering that Western constitutional democracy is rooted in and to some extent dependent on basic religious and philosophical convictions which are not to be found in many of the developing countries. Many, indeed most of the communities that have adopted constitutions in this century are not Christian communities. Nor do they share the heritage of Roman law and Greek philosophy. The very thought processes upon which Western constitutionalism rests are part of this tradition. Aristotelian logic is involved in one of the central doctrines of this constitutionalism; as none other than Kant pointed out, the separation of powers is based upon distinctions which resemble the figures of traditional Western logic.

CARL J. FRIEDRICH's *career as a political scientist stretches over five decades and includes the Presidency of the American Political Science Association and the Vice Presidency of the International Political Science Association. He has written on political theory, comparative government, philosophy, history, jurisprudence, and recently, in his* Man and His Government *(1963), on developing areas, with particular reference to Africa.*

9

Every state (*civitas*) contains three powers, that is the general, united will in threefold personality (*trias politica*): the ruling power (sovereignty) in that of the legislative, the executive power in that of the governor (according to law) and the judicial power, attributing to each what is his according to law, in the person of the judge. . . . They are like the three propositions in a practical syllogism of reason: the first major premise which gives the rule of the will, the minor second premise which provides the command of how to proceed according to law, i.e. the principle of how to subsume it under the first major premise, and the conclusion which contains the judgment as to what is law in the instant case.[1]

I – The Heritage of Constitutionalism

In more modern parlance, the matter may be cast in terms of decision-making. The power to command involves the ability to decide. There are general and specific decisions, and the latter may be instances of the former. Specific decisions are the realm of the executive power; general decisions belong to the sphere of the legislative or rule-making power. The judicial power stands between the two; it transforms a general into a specific decision.[2] Now according to this syndrome of decision-making, it is clear that most of the time both the conclusion and the minor premise will be provided by the executive, while the judicial, when it is called into the play, in actual fact reexamines whether the subsumption made by the party on trial was rightly made—what Kant in keeping with his thinking in terms of constitutional rule of law (*Rechtsstaat*) assumed was the judicial power's preoccupation with checking the acts of the executive. A political system based upon the assumption of the universal validity and the universal discernment of such premises will tend to break down where such propositions are not at all understood or accepted.[3] This kind of problem is at the heart of F. S. C. Northrop's well known work on the divergent thought processes of East and West, and more especially the emphasis on the "intuitive aesthetic character" of Oriental thought. The nonana-

---

[1] Kant, *Rechtslehre*, para. 45.
[2] See for this my *Constitutional Government and Democracy* (1950), pp. 185-86.
[3] The problem resembles that of the non-Euclidian geometries in modern science; unfortunately the problem of non-Aristotelian logics has not received any systematic exploration, except to note their existence.

lytic, nondiscursive "teachings" of Confucian, Buddhist, and Vedic political thought are epigrammatic and hence intuitive.[4]

The difficulties arising from these convictional and cognitional contrasts and divergencies have led many to the opposite extreme of maintaining that the political theory developed in the West is completely inapplicable to this new world. Such a complete relativism, to some extent derived from the misunderstood relativism of cultural anthropology,[5] is incompatible with the spirit of science and the fundamental premise of all genuine theory. For such theory presupposes that there is one truth, and that the appearance of relativity is due to failure to observe and properly account for differentiating factors. To put it another way, it is as important for the youth of developing countries of non-European background to study Aristotle as it is for ours, even more so. The inadequacy of some of the formalistic statements of Western political science, derived from particular legal systems of the West, ought not to be allowed to lead to a rejection of a general political science.

The numerous striking propositions which political theory offers concerning power, rule, and influence are, of course, applicable to developing countries; if they were not, they would not be true generalizations. Thus the proposition that power is generated by both consent and constraint, that constraint (or coercion) has three primary forms—physical, economic, and psychic—as has consent, and that from consent springs political leadership, these and many similar regularities which political science has studied and continues to elucidate apply to developing countries. Indeed, they help to make evident that in many basic aspects the politics of developing countries is not at all different from the politics, the drama of leadership and followership, in highly developed communities.

II – Are Constitutionalist Principles Inapplicable?

To illustrate, surely Max Weber's celebrated threefold division of legitimacy into a traditional, a rational-legal, and a charismatic one[6] is meant to be applicable and is in fact quite meaningful in dealing

---

[4] F. S. C. Northrop, *The Meeting of East and West—An Inquiry Concerning World Understanding* (1946). See also *The Wisdom of Confucius,* ed. and trans. by Lin Yutang (1943).

[5] See Clyde Kluckhohn, *A Mirror for Man* (1949) for competent and searching professional criticism of this position. See also my *Man and His Government* (1963) for much of what follows.

[6] Max Weber, *Wirtschaft und Gesellshaft* (1921), Chap. III.

with the political orders of emergent countries. The basis of legitimacy of the present governments of Ethiopia, Egypt, and Saudi Arabia, to take three examples at random, may be distinguished according to the Weberian triad, though numerous difficulties present themselves as to detail. These Weber would seek to minimize by claiming that the three categories were "ideal types" and hence could not be tested by concrete examples except in an approximate way.[7] But whether ideal-typical or not, and whether exhaustive or not, these concepts provide meaningful analytical tools for the study of non-Western political orders, because tradition, law, and rationality are "panhuman" categories, that is, they apply to all men.

To continue the argument a step further, surely the universal trend to make constitutions is the manifestation of the need and an expression of a search for some kind of democratic legitimacy.[8] Max Weber would perhaps have argued that it is the result of a widely felt need of rational-legal legitimation, because of the breakdown of tradition and the absence of charismatic leadership. Legitimacy is the proper term for designating the political constellation in which a ruler is believed by those he rules to have a right to do so (and this includes in the present world also to some extent the belief of those not ruled by him, but participants in the international order, such as it is). Hence a "constitution," no matter how unrealistic in the sense of being nondescriptive of who actually governs, has a certain value.[9] Indeed, even a constitution which is least satisfactory from the point of view of guaranteeing the observance of its rules, especially those meant to protect the private individual, is apt to contain numerous provisions which do describe actual governmental practice. Thus the Constitution of the Soviet Union, while certainly a façade in many ways, contains a rational-legal pattern and therefore legitimizes the rulers to a certain extent, in the eyes of Soviet citizens and of the world at large.

Besides providing a measure of legitimacy for the rulers of a new state, a constitution is also a symbol of national unity. Like the

---

[7] For this see my *Man and His Government* (1963), Note 2. The serious objections to the "charismatic" notion are explored in Chap. X, and in my article in the *Journal of Politics*, XXIII (1961), 3ff.

[8] Guiglielmo Ferrero, *The Principles of Power* (1942), employs this term. For legitimacy see my *Man and His Government* (1963), Chap. 13.

[9] See G. Sartori, "Constitutionalism: A Preliminary Discussion," in *American Political Science Review*, LVI (Dec. 1962), 853-64, and the critique by W. H. Morris-Jones, "On Constitutionalism," *ibid.*, LIX (June 1965), 439-44, with rejoinder by Sartori.

flag, it is a unifying and hence integrating symbol, often implying or indeed explicating a foundation myth. The symbolism and the implied myth are suggesting that a new person has come into being, a collective entity has been born. How otherwise could a constituent power have been operating to create the constitution? The constituent power is closely related to the cataclysmic advent of a revolution, in this case, a colonial revolution. After such a revolution the constituent power is wielded by a constituent group which, no matter how small or large, sets up a government. According to the democratic ideology which inspired it, the revolution ought to be democratic. Hence the compelling need to organize the community under a democratic constitution. This compulsion worked even in the case of the Soviet Union, it will be remembered, although there is nothing to be found in Marx about the need or desirability of a constitution. For him, "justice is a bourgeois prejudice," and so is law. But the new nations, inspired by Rousseau's passionate teachings (not always directly, of course) deeply feel the need of manifesting their nationhood in a constituent act. Hence the constitution is made to form both symbol and myth.[10] As Edward Shils has commented, "Ever since the American Revolution, the act of creating a state has tended to entail the declaration of the fundamental law of the new country in the form of a constitution. The process of constitution-making has been regarded as a major *symbol* of the formation of the new state." [11]

The task of integrating often very disparate elements resulting from colonial conquest and held together by colonial rule is perhaps the most pressing need of all the new states. When one speaks in those cases of "emergent nations," he gainsays the large amount of human effort that has to be expended in order to bring this "emergence" about. And the attempts at constitution-making are part of that gigantic effort.

III – Nations and Nationalism

Western constitutionalism was instituted only after nations had come into being, and the core of a common government, more espe-

[10] On the constituent power, see my *Constitutional Government and Democracy*, Chaps. VII and VIII. It is there shown why the constituent power must neither be confused with the amending power nor be superseded by it.

[11] Edward Shils, "The Fortunes of Constitutional Government in the Political Development of the New States," in John Hallowell, ed., *Development: For What?* (Durham, N.C.: Duke University Press, 1964), p. 104. Italics added.

cially a functioning administrative service, had been organized. We hear a great deal nowadays about "nation-building." [12] It is important, therefore, to recall that the nations of Europe were not built, but formed in the course of a long historic process. The fact that Western nations were not built, but grew, may be an important reason why a predominantly analytic political science could develop in the West. By contrast, the need for prescriptive propositions is very great in developing countries, and the analytic approach does not suit their needs.[13] Even the modern nation-state, the political order of such a nation, was not deliberately built, but rather came into being as expansionist rulers sought to strengthen their government. These modern European nation-states were a very distinctive kind of political order, ultimately dependent upon an *in*clusive religious community which was Christian, and an *ex*clusive secular community which was national. The growth of Western nations was undoubtedly facilitated by the prevalence of one unifying religion, even if it was split into various denominations. Some of the appeal of Communism is derived from the fact that it provides a secular substitute. The "thought control" developed in Communist China is based upon this pseudoreligious appeal and its unifying political potentialities.

This appeal rests in part upon the rise and fall of imperialism. In our time, when the idea of a nation-state has become moribund in the West, this same idea has become a worldwide goal of peoples who, having shaken off colonial rule, have adopted "nationalism." This nationalism, while rapidly eroding in Europe where a more inclusive idea of European unity is superseding it, has in fact been hammered into a kind of ideology in many new countries where the making of a nation is not only a task of great practical difficulty,

---

[12] See Karl Deutsch and Williams J. Foltz, eds., *Nation-Building* (New York: Atherton Press, 1963); Rupert Emerson, *From Empire to Nation* (New York: 1960).

[13] See for this my paper "The Nation: Growth or Artifact?" read to the Florence meeting of the Institut International de Philosophie Politique, July 1965, and published in their *Annales* (1966). The writing on the new nations in Asia, Africa, and elsewhere is, of course, full of divergent data. For an overview see the interesting study by John H. Kautsky, "An Essay in the Politics of Development" in the volume edited by him and entitled *Political Change in Underdeveloped Countries* (1963), pp. 3-119; the particular discussion of nationalism is on pp. 30-57. See also James S. Coleman's study "Nationalism in Africa," *ibid.*, pp. 167-94, and Joel Carmichael's "The National-Communist Symbiosis in the Middle East," *ibid.*, pp. 304-15.

but fraught with intellectual problems resulting from older traditions.[14] Ancient orders in these countries are rapidly disintegrating, if they have not already been totally destroyed. At the same time, the national state is being preached as the panacea for solving the problems of a new political order. Vast heterogeneous populations united by some tenuous cultural bond, like India, are referred to as "nations," as are tribal conglomerates such as the Congo. These entities, whatever their political future, surely are not the same as Western nations. Yet as constituents of the United Nations, these peoples are legally endowed with "nationhood." Surely this development calls for a broader concept of the nation than has been shaped by the past of Europe. Empirically and pragmatically a nation today is any cohesive group possessing independence within the confines of an international order, as defined by the United Nations. But it is a nation only if it provides a constituency for a government effectively ruling such a group and legitimized by it. Folk tradition, religion, and other related factors contribute to cohesiveness; they are not decisive for the nation's existence.[15]

If what I have said is right, then the forming of nations is in the contemporary world indeed a task of building a whole by integrating disparate parts. Such a nation's being is in fact constituted by a founding act. It is very much more political in the strict modern sense, very much less cultural in the old European sense. Hence the paramount urgency of a constitution. Such a constitution defines a regime; it institutionalizes a pattern of power relations, more especially identifying the lead group, the elite. If it is to work, it must function effectively in forwarding integration and in providing a

[14] Robert R. Bowie and Associates, *United States Foreign Policy: Ideology and Foreign Affairs* (Washington, D.C.: Government Printing Office, 1959).

[15] See my *Man and His Government*, Chap. 30. Herbert J. Spiro, in his interesting essay on "The Primacy of Political Development" in his *Africa: The Primacy of Politics* (1966), p. 166, suggests that national integration "in the conventional meaning of the term, is not an important goal of most leadership groups in African states." This seems to me to run against a great deal of evidence, hardly to be outweighed by the data Thomas Hovet has gathered, enlightening as they are, about "African Politics in the United Nations," *ibid.*, pp. 116-49.

See also Lucian W. Pye, *Politics, Personality, and Nation Building: Burma's Search for Identity* (1962), which interprets modernization as "nation-building"; see especially his Chaps. II and III, "Analytical Approaches to Nation Building" and "The Nature of Transitional Politics." The problem of nation-building is here outlined "in the context . . . of the form of political process characteristic of transitional societies in general" (p. 32).

sense of selfhood, of identity. The community may be actual or potential. In any case, it results from the constitution rather than being presupposed by it. But can Western constitutionalism provide the models?

IV – *The Historical Background of Constitutionalism*

Western constitutionalism is a complex product of Western culture.[16] It slowly evolved in response to the problem of government in a Christian society. This problem is a particular aspect of the more general problem of what distinguishes the Western from other cultures. Max Weber stressed five factors as of primary significance in Western culture: (1) liberation of thought from magic, (2) separation of church and state, (3) emergence of an urban middle class, (4) development of modern central bureaucracy (state), and (5) economic rationality.[17] Weber's stress on bureaucracy, while very sound in itself, is misleading when it is not linked with the growth of constitutionalism. To be sure, such constitutionalizing presupposes the establishment of a bureaucracy, the core of the modern state, but the modern state is not fully developed until that bureaucracy has been made "responsible," i.e., constitutionalized. The long line of thinkers from Machiavelli through Bodin and Hobbes to Montesquieu, Kant, and Hegel in fact were all more concerned, theoretically, with the problem of constitutionalism and its relation to the state than with the activities of the bureaucracy which was growing up all around them. The challenge of "sovereignty" was essentially born of these concerns with the state and its constitution. "The state" Bodin had described as the government of an association of families, and to be well ordered he thought it required a single sovereign, that is to say, a person or group of persons who possess supreme legislative power. The focus of attention, hence, was on legislation rather than administration. While the bureaucracy had the decisive hand in legislation under monarchical absolutism, the sanctity of the law and the halo surrounding all lawgiving greatly reinforced association of the rational with the legal and the consequent rise of constitutionalism. Sanctioned by general

[16] Carl J. Friedrich, *Transcendent Justice—The Religious Foundations of Constitutionalism* (Durham, N.C.: Duke University Press, 1964).

[17] There is a similar summation in Lowenthal, cited below, footnote 31, pp. 182-84, but I think that Weber places the stress on Western dynamism rather than culture in general.

propositions of Greek philosophy and Roman law, the conviction became predominant that government itself must be conducted according to law, and that such law must be embodied in a constitution.

V – Rights and Their Enforcement

This conviction was greatly strengthened, and perhaps even originally inspired, by the Christian belief in the dignity of every human person, and by the equally Christian conviction of the sinfulness of power and its allurements. Like sex, political power is intensely human, but both are morally suspect and liable to perversion and abuse. The felt need for a constitution was also a projection of the legalism which Rome and Israel had believed in: the belief that goodness is the result of obeying rules framed by reason in the light of human frailty and in response to divine instruction. As a result, this extraordinary constitutionalist concept of political order possesses two focal points. The first of these is a firm guarantee of basic rights, or liberties, or freedoms,[18] as they have been successively called in the course of their evolution and universalization. For starting as the rights of Englishmen or Spaniards—in other words, of distinctive national groups and indeed of limited classes such as barons and knights—they gradually became generalized in theory and practice until they finally were applied to the world at large. It has been claimed that in Africa too there is a kind of recognition of "fundamental and inalienable rights," because most traditional African societies were based upon three principles, custom, justice or morality, and divine law. But these three principles were circumscribed in terms germane to each society, and "there was little or no sense of freedom of thought or religion; a tribesman had to accept the tribal religion as he found it." At the same time, it was admitted that "the concept of an opposition . . . was completely unknown." From these statements it is clear that the basis of human rights, namely freedom of conviction, was definitely absent.[19]

Whereas within the European context the notion of such rights,

[18] See my "Rights, Liberties, Freedoms: A Reappraisal," in *The American Political Science Review*, LVII (1963), 841-54; also "Chrestomathie des Droits de l'Homme," *Politique—Revue Internationale des Doctrines et des Institutions* (1960), Nos. 10-13.

[19] Antony Allott, "The African Conception of the Rule of Law" in Hallowell, ed., *op. cit.*, pp. 98-99.

liberties, and freedoms has remained linked to the essential requirement of enforcement machinery, the understanding of this vital
ingredient has been lacking in many of the subsequent followers of
the philosophy of rights. The contrast is strikingly illustrated by the
fact that whereas the European Declaration of Human Rights was
supplemented by enforcement machinery, namely the European
Commission of Human Rights,[20] the General Declaration of Human Rights of the United Nations has so far not been provided with
anything similar, nor is there any near prospect that it will be.

The notion of such enforcement machinery has ancient roots. In
their speculations about ideal or model political orders, the Greek
philosophers had already hit upon the notion of the mixed constitution, compounded of several distinct elements in the interest of
justice, happiness, and stability. Elaborated by Polybius and revived
by Machiavelli and his numerous followers, the notion was eventually transformed into that of a separation of powers. While familiar
enough in the history of political thought, the separation of powers
has not received the needed attention from most of the men engaged
in making constitutions for newly emergent states. This is in part
due to the fact that it was and is widely believed that the British
parliamentary system superseded the separation of powers, when as
a matter of fact it exchanged a crude and simple for a subtle and
complex system of divided powers.[21] It has also often been argued
that the separation of powers was "annulled" by the growth of the
party system which, it is said, reintegrated and reconcentrated what
had been separated and divided. Fortunately or unfortunately, this
is by no means true. Due to American federalism, itself a kind of
spatial or territorial division of powers,[22] parties in America are
deeply divided and thus provide that safeguard against concen-
tration of power which the maintenance of basic right calls for, not
to mention the clear and constitutionally entrenched separation of
the judiciary, as epitomized in the Supreme Court. Clearly then,
the Western tradition of constitutionalism not only proclaims basic
rights, but it also protects them through machinery which subtly

---

[20] D. P. Myers, "The European Commission of Human Rights," *American
Journal of International Law*, L (1956); A. H. Robertson, "The European Court
of Human Rights," *International and Comparative Law Quarterly* (1959).

[21] See my *Constitutional Government and Democracy*, Chaps. X and XI.

[22] See my "New Tendencies in Federal Theory and Practice," in *Jahrbuch des
Oeffentlichen Rechts*, XIV (1965), 1ff., and Arthur Maass, ed., *Area and Power*
(1959).

balances the three basic functions of settling disputes, making rules, and taking measures to enforce the rules and settlements. The conventional wisdom of dividing political power among three human agencies—the executive, the legislative, and the judicial—has been in both theory and practice expressed in a great variety of particular constitutions. Europe and America have proliferated such constitutions since the first prototypes were attempted in Italian and German communes and were afterwards, especially since the middle of the seventeenth century, elaborated first in England and then on the Continent. Such constitutional orders, revolving at first around the freedom of religion and the right of property, smoothed the path toward that unique achievement of the West, constitutional democracy, resembling in some ways the mixed forms of government which Aristotle, Polybius, and Cicero had celebrated. But whereas stability had been the watchword of the Ancients in their approach to political order, it now became freedom and social justice for all.

VI – *Are Constitutions Suitable for a Developing Economy?*

Is it reasonable to expect that the developing countries in one great leap forward not only adopt such constitutions but also make them work? Can they hope, without firm anchorage in the Judaeo-Christian religious heritage, to operate a developing economy in so complex a fashion? Are not the European nations themselves finding the machinery of constitutionalism increasingly difficult to manipulate as they face an ever more highly developed industrial economy and the rising expectations of its urban masses? Are emergent countries not bound to abandon the distinctively Western kind of constitutionalism in favor of a more integrated and more communally directed order? The Constitutions of the Soviet Union, Poland and other Communist regimes, surely no embodiments of Western constitutionalism, seem to many to provide a more suitable framework for the tasks of development and national integration. Thus Red China operates with power concentrated in the hands of the lead group, who are fired by a missionary zeal for an abiding faith in themselves as the true providers of a better future. In all those communities where there is little suspicion of power and scant demand for personal rights and liberties—their past religions having had no particular concern with either—concentrated power seems to many the answer to the pressing problems of development.[23]

It has always seemed a bit curious that the fate which has overtaken so many of the constitutions in quite a few emergent states should have come as a surprise to so many of their architects. After all, Latin America has had long experience with comparable situations. There constitutions, usually modeled on the American *Vorbild* or paradigm, have regularly been flouted and set aside by military juntas, practically without exception. But of course this history was treated as nonexemplary and hence irrelevant. This may be due in part to the fact that the constitutions of the new states were largely of the parliamentary type. They were modeled on the paradigm of the parliamentary systems of Britain, as well as Ireland, the Netherlands, France, and others. This was no doubt the consequence of the education and training of the leaders of the independence movements, who, in spite of their hostility to their colonial masters, tended to look to them for guidance in the matter of political practice. Since they are powerful, so the argument runs, they must know how to run governments. In addition, the expert advisers of new regimes were quite often strong believers in parliamentary democracy—men like Sir Ivor Jennings, for example—as were of course the officials in the colonial offices who usually guided the preliminary steps taken before independence. Even in countries with a long constitutional tradition of their own, such as Germany, this factor played a role.

The notion of a constitutional democracy was in the minds of leaders and their constituents alike somewhat vague and often confused with that of a radical democracy in the continental tradition of Rousseau.[24] While there was a general readiness to recognize the importance of limiting the exercise of governmental power and of

[23] Gabriel A. Almond and James S. Coleman, eds., *The Politics of the Developing Areas* (New York: 1960). There is a growing literature on one-party regimes. See Clement H. Moore's *Tunisia Since Independence: The Dynamics of One-Party Government* (1965), which considerably diverges from his "The National Party: A Tentative Model," *Public Policy*, X (1960), 239ff. See also the comments in his chapter in the work edited by Herbert J. Spiro, *Africa: The Primacy of Politics*.

[24] This lack of a clearly defined concept of constitutionalism mars the otherwise very broadly suggestive discussion of Shils, *op. cit.*, with which I find myself nonetheless in general agreement. I am not always sure, however, what the bearing of particular comments is, since other basic terms such as *legitimacy*, *authority*, and *charismatic* are equivocal, though presumably their meaning is derived by Shils from Max Weber, of whom he is a close student.

permitting free expression of opinion in regard to politics, there was an equally strong conviction that the majority's preferences should prevail. As a result, these systems tended to evolve rather rapidly toward a crisis, a critical conflict over which was more important, the constitution or the will of the people. In most countries the constitution once adopted has been left as it was adopted, even though actual practice has tended to depart ever more markedly from the original form and intent. And although there was at first a tendency to avoid its abrogation, the readiness to do so has recently increased. Not only in Pakistan and Indonesia, but in Nigeria, Ghana, and other African states the constitution has not only been violated, but in fact suspended. Even when the un- and anticonstitutional practices have not been carried quite that far, there has been a fairly widespread disregard for some of the most significant constitutional (i.e., basic) rights and little if any respect for the necessary enforcement machinery, especially the existence of an organized opposition. Such an opposition is, under more recent party systems, the crucial equivalent of the older separation of powers. As already mentioned, it constitutes in a sense a new separation of powers in sequence (time) replacing the conventional separation in function (space). Something more will be said on this score presently. But let us first note here that the constitutional violations have included censoring of the press and imprisoning of journalists and writers, persecution and even suppression of racial, religious, and linguistic (cultural) minorities, and of course elimination and forcible amalgamation of opposition parties. There exists always and in any constitutional regime a certain spread between norm and actual performance; indeed, what has been called the living constitution has always differed from what is written in constitutional charters and statute books. But it would obviously be absurd to speak of a living constitution when in fact the very basic characteristic of a constitutional order is no longer operative, that is to say, when its regularized restraint of governmental power in the interest of protecting a personal sphere of the individual citizen and his voluntary associations is destroyed.[25] This tendency is unfortunately

[25] The confusion of thought on this score is the direct result of arguing about the role of constitutionalism without a clearly defined understanding of what constitutional government means. See Herbert J. Spiro, *Government by Constitution—The Political Systems of Democracy* (1959), which, in spite of its many insightful explorations of constitutional issues, lacks such a definition. However, its meaning emerges in the course of the work and is epitomized on the brief discussion of "The Model Constitution," pp. 437-40.

encouraged by the fact that the so-called constitutions which have been put forth in the Soviet Union and other totalitarian regimes have obscured the basic issue. If the constitution is seen as an instrument of class warfare, it obviously is something different from the democratic and personalist constitution defined above. "The basic task of the Constitution is the establishment of the dictatorship of the city and village proletariat," one reads in the Soviet Constitution of 1918. As such it cannot be simply discarded as "mere façade," for every constitution contains strong ideological elements. Not only any bill of rights it may contain, but also the organizational features it fixes are ideologically determined.[26] But if the term *constitution* is employed in such a generalized sense (customary since Aristotle's discussion of the *politeia,* a term which is usually rendered as *constitution*), then a prefix such as *liberal, democratic,* or *personalist* ought to indicate that one is speaking of this specifically Western constitution. And since Western constitutionalism in the tradition of British political theorists from Fortescue to Locke provides the archetype of this notion, it may even be sensible to speak of a "constitutionalist" constitution. (Terms like *genuine, real,* and the like have too pejorative an implication.)

VII – Succession and the Constituent Power

It has been a key feature of "constitutionalist" constitutions to provide for succession on a regularly recurrent basis, this recurrency having an important restraining influence. It is lacking in the totalitarian constitutions. It has also been the Achilles heel of many of the new constitutions. Assassination has, of course, no particular institutional significance; else we would have to question the constitutionalist character of the American order. Yet, when such assassination is the precursor of revolutionary and counterrevolutionary transformations in the political order, it attains symptomatic significance for the weakness of constitutionalism. In Pakistan, Iraq, Syria, and South Vietnam, as in Nigeria and in many Latin American countries, such assassination has been the harbinger of a breakdown of the constitutional system.

[26] For a fuller exploration of these problems see the new Chap. X in Carl J. Friedrich and Zbigniew Brzezinski, *Totalitarian Dictatorship and Autocracy,* 2nd ed. (1965). The suggestion that such constitutions are mere façade is made with special emphasis by G. Sartori in his "Constitutionalism: A Preliminary Discussion," *American Political Science Review,* LVI (1962), 853ff. It has been recurrent in recent writing, e.g., Spiro, *Government by Constitution, op. cit.*

More significant, though closely related, have been the military coups. Latin America apart, there have been such coups in Indonesia, Burma, Pakistan, Sudan, Turkey, Iraq, Syria, Egypt, South Korea, Laos, Togo, Algeria, Nigeria, Ghana, and elsewhere. Attempted coups would lengthen the list; every few months a new country is added to it. As was remarked earlier, such military coups seem the characteristic alternative to a constitutionalist regime when traditional orders have broken down beyond revival and when totalitarian, especially Communist, alternatives are rejected by military and related elites. The ensuing regimes are at times more "liberal" than the preceding regime—liberal, that is, in the sense of allowing a somewhat broader spectrum of opinion to be expressed. At the same time "the military are, in fact, much like the civilian politicians they displace." [27]

Besides certain other motivations (and conditions) of military takeover, the breakdown of the constitutionalist regime as manifested in civil war plays a vital role, and not only in new emergent countries—Spain is a striking example. Civil war is endemic in constitutionalism, especially where a rampant pluralism is reinforced and given institutional escapes through federalism (to be considered presently). Unless, therefore, societies already possess a certain homogeneity, the risks involved in its adoption are very great. A number of emergent countries, notably the Congo, Indonesia, Iraq, Korea, and Vietnam, have been involved in civil war; others like India are threatened by it, with flareups here and there highlighting the danger. Military takeovers have been motivated and rationalized as anticipating such developments. It was a crucial factor in the return to power in 1958 of General de Gaulle, who, however, in turn stopped the further expansion of military power. Usually pragmatic in outlook, military men cannot cope with a civil war situation without seeking some kind of legitimation, but the legitimizing force of constitutionalism is becoming weaker. Even so, regimes like that of General Ky in South Vietnam have once again,

[27] Shils, *op. cit.* p. 129. Shils adds: "The fact is that government by the military in some respects brings to a more open expression certain of the political aspirations of those they displace and of those over whom they exercise power." For the role of the military see also the informative volume edited by John J. Johnson, *The Role of the Military in Underdeveloped Countries* (1962), covering Latin America, Indonesia, Burma, Thailand, the Middle East, and Africa, with a broad introductory essay by Shils. For an excellent case study see Richard D. Robinson, *The First Turkish Republic: A Case Study in National Development* (1963), especially Chap. IX.

like Latin American dictatorships, sought to exploit the democratic and popular implications of constitutionalism.

The difficulty is, however, that military and related elites do not in any substantive sense constitute a constituent group. The constituent power mentioned before is another ill-understood dimension of the constitutionalist tradition. Restating an original Lockean normative proposition in descriptive terms, based on much constitutionalist experience, I described the constituent group some years ago as one which consists of a considerable number of the more vital and intelligent men who, animated by a desire for freedom, are determined to organize a constitutionalist regime. Unless this purpose is dominant, no constituent group exists; therefore one might say that in most emergent countries these groups were feeble and have since disappeared, for an elite group which seeks merely power or the establishment of a totalitarian system is not a constituent group.[28]

VIII – Emergency Power and Dictatorship

The disappearance of constituent groups is not surprising in view of the successive breakdowns and performance failures of constitutionalist orders. It has at times been rather impressively argued both inside and outside the developing countries that the reason constitutionalism has no application to them is that they are living in a state of permanent emergency. They plead that even developed constitutional systems recognize that under the stress of crisis the regular procedures are suspended and the country lives under a system of constitutional dictatorship.[29] It is very true that the United States, Great Britain, and other constitutional democracies have developed fairly elaborate institutions under the general heading of emergency powers and related terms, such as state of siege, martial

[28] See my *Constitutional Government and Democracy* (1950), Chap. VIII. Within the context of a suggestive application of the Hegelian dialectic of master and servant, Clement Henry Moore, in his study "Mass Party Regimes in Africa" in Herbert Spiro, ed., *Africa: The Primacy of Politics*, pp. 99-104, delineates the emergence of a *"pays réel,"* an organized political system before independence is actually achieved. Significantly, the nationalist rather than the constitutionalist thrust is in the foreground of attention.

[29] For an elaboration of this concept and how it fits into constitutional theory, see my *Constitutional Government and Democracy*, Chap. XXVI. The argument has been advanced, for example, by Nyerere in connection with his defense of one-party systems and the nonrecognition of an opposition.

law, etc. But two things ought to be borne in mind in order not to
misjudge this aspect of constitutionalism. First, the exercise of
emergency powers is itself hedged in by detailed provisions,[30] and
second, the constitution remains in force, and the activities it pre-
scribes can therefore be resumed the moment the emergency passes.
This is what happened in the United States in 1918 and 1945, as
it did in Britain at the same time. It is part of such continuance of
the constitutional order that in fact only certain limited parts of
this order are suspended during the emergency; much else goes on
as usual. The United States during the Civil War, no less than during the two world wars, not only kept Congress operating but maintained the two-party system and indeed held general elections. The
argument is therefore not tenable in its general form, though there
can be no doubt that the existence of an emergency (namely, the
need for rapid economic development in the face of hunger) affects
constitutional operations. But it is doubtful whether an emergency
requires some kind of "development dictatorship" for the solution
of the tasks confronting the country, as has at times been argued.[31]
The developing countries are not facing the early stages of Western
political development, but rather different developmental patterns
which, while starting in response to Western models, are molded
by a great variety of different conditions. It is particularly risky to
argue, as is sometimes done, out of the European background and
to suggest that since constitutional government in Europe arose out
of a background of absolutist and tyrannical regimes the same might
happen in Asia and Africa. Not only is the history of European
constitutionalism by no means that simple, but such a statement
largely neglects the positive forces that went into the making of
constitutional government in Europe.[32]

[30] The long-drawn-out struggle in the Federal Republic of Germany over how
to structure this field of constitutional law, still going on, provides an illuminat-
ing illustration of this side of the matter.

[31] For the term *development dictatorship* see Richard Lowenthal, "Government in the Developing Countries—Its Functions and Forms" in Henry W.
Ehrmann, ed., *Democracy in a Changing Society*, p. 206, and reprinted as a
separate study by the School of International Affairs at Columbia University.

[32] See Carl J. Friedrich, *Transcendent Justice—The Religious Foundations of
Constitutionalism.* See also such classical studies as J. G. A. Pocock, *The Ancient
Constitution and the Feudal Law—English Historical Thought in the Seventeenth
Century* (1957), and Charles H. McIlwain, *The High Court of Parliament and
Its Supremacy* (1910). Pocock rightly stresses that the common law tradition
retained the medieval "almost universally respected doctrine that the law
should be above will" (p. 51). See also the statement that "it was natural that

IX – A Counter-Case: Puerto Rico

It is interesting at this point to ponder the fact that constitutional development in Puerto Rico has traversed a course very divergent from that of most ex-colonial countries. After a period of considerable violence this once "desperate isle" has emerged as an autonomous state within the confines of the United States Constitution. It was able to construct and maintain a constitutionalist regime of considerable vitality and apparent durability, because within the framework of a broadly planned economic prosperity and rapidly rising standard of living Puerto Rico could build on the spiritual heritage presupposed by Western constitutionalism. Its homogeneous Spanish-speaking and Catholic-Christian population readily responded to the implicit values and beliefs. After all, medieval Spanish constitutionalism, embodied in the battle cry of Spain's free cities, the *fuero fundamental,* was their own heritage.[33]

This middle road to freedom was opened up by an exceptional colonial administrator who, animated by fervent democratic convictions, came to realize that only responsible self-government would provide the kind of inspiration and leadership which, when adequately supported, might improve the condition of the desperate isle.[34] The political instrumentality of this transformation became the Popular Democratic Party (PPD), led by an outstanding inspirational leader, Luis Muñoz Marin. The PPD has dominated the political life of Puerto Rico to such an extent that the minority parties have had to be protected by special constitutional devices. These

---

those who sought to defend threatened privileges or liberties should emphasize in return that their rights were rooted in a law which no king could invade" (p. 16). It is obvious that the starting point here was diametrically the opposite one from that now being reached in the emergent countries.

[33] See my *Puerto Rico—Middle Road to Freedom: Fuero Fundamental* (1959), and the literature cited there. Since that publication several important studies have greatly deepened our understanding of the underlying belief-structure. See especially Robert W. Anderson, *Party Politics in Puerto Rico* (1965); Gordon K. Lewis, *Puerto Rico* (1963); and the several studies put out by the United States–Puerto Rico Commission on the Status of Puerto Rico, especially Robert H. Hunter, *Historical Survey of the Puerto Rico Status Question, 1898-1965* (1965), and Sidney W. Mintz, *Puerto Rico—An Essay in the Definition of a National Culture* (1965).

[34] Rexford Tugwell, *The Stricken Land* (1947), *passim,* and the skillful appraisal of Tugwell's role in Charles T. Goodsell, *Administration of Revolution —Executive Reform in Puerto Rico Under Governor Rexford Tugwell, 1941-1946* (1965).

devices, which give them greater representation than their votes justify, are the obverse of what can usually be observed in Latin American, African, and Asian politics, where, as already noted, opposition is very generally hampered, if not altogether suppressed. Muñoz Marin always remained alert to the danger of "personalism" and successfully advocated various means of strengthening the opposition, especially in the matter of party finance, where the lesser opposition parties receive the same amount of government funds as the ruling party. Yet, the enthusiasm of his following was such that he had the greatest difficulty in extricating himself from the governorship. In a dramatic meeting he faced a shouting crowd demonstrating against his decision not to run again. He wanted the Puerto Rican electorate to become "mature." Only very recently had the party taken formal steps to institutionalize and depersonalize its authority. Rightly, its best informed student commented that this was "a momentous step," adding that "while Muñoz remained the party's fountainhead and symbol of authority, it is highly doubtful whether any real movement to institutionalize the party was possible." [35] Muñoz Martin has now stepped down, and the transformation is under way. It is to some extent a matter of generations; as young voters who have been born under the new order of the Free and Associated Commonwealth come of age, the electorate is increasingly apt to take things for granted which formerly were "ideological" and disputed.[36] Even the cherished *hispanidad* of the earlier days is somewhat fading. But what remains is the sediment of convictions derived from a Christian past which is manifest in the nearly universal background of Catholicism.

X – Federalism

The Puerto Rican case suggests a brief return to the problem of federalism, for her association with the United States constitutes a looser federal bond than that prevailing in the Union. Federalism needs to be understood, as is now increasingly the case, not only as a pattern or design for dividing powers between two levels of government but also as a process of federalizing, that is to say, an ongoing evolution towards either greater unity or greater diversity. But whatever the approach, whether static or dynamic, federalism

[35] Robert W. Anderson, *op. cit.* p. 222.
[36] Ismael R. Bou, *Esbozo de un tema—Las Nuevas Generaciones en Puerto Rico* (1963).

presupposes constitutionalism. Only where the notion of autonomous spheres for individual and group is understood and believed
in, where therefore the notion of restraints upon governmental action for the purpose of protecting such spheres is grasped and af-
firmed, can federalism be durable. The hope that one can employ it
merely as a gadget, a mechanism for resolving group antagonism
and conflict, as in Nigeria and elsewhere, is doomed at the outset.
The history of Switzerland is a striking instance of where the moor-
ings of federalizing procedure as an ongoing process must be sought.
As a recent analyst has poignantly remarked: "A peasant from
Appenzell, a socialist worker from Berne and an anglophile banker
from Geneva . . . do not have much to say to each other, but they
know that they are attached to the same political institutions, to
the same common rules arranged so as to allow them to remain different. . . . But the three know that they are Swiss, not because of
some common quality, either natural or cultural, but because they
are placed in the same *ensemble* which is called Switzerland which
they approve. If one has understood that, he has understood federalism." [37] It is clear that such an attitude of tolerance for diver-
gence and indeed contrast presupposes a belief in the dignity and
hence the convictional autonomy of every man, a belief which rests
upon a submerged, even hidden religious faith.

What the component units of a federal order then claim and seek
to achieve or maintain is autonomy, institutionalized in and guaranteed by a living constitution. In the United States there has been
increasing talk of "creative" federalism as contrasted with what is
sometimes called "restrictive" federalism. Such creative federalism
emphasizes the partnership of national and local authorities. It involves, we are told, "both cooperation and competition of ideas
and performance between all levels of government." [38] Such creative
federalism would, of course, seem to fit better the tasks with which
emergent countries are confronted. Its reliance on joint effort, joint
planning, and so on sounds very appropriate. But when one learns
that it means neither giving the national government predomi-
nance nor increasing local dependence upon national financial support, but rather accepting the expanding role of state and local gov-

[37] Denis de Rougemont, *La Suisse—ou l'histoire d'un peuple heureaux* (1965),
pp. 112-13. See also Kenneth D. McRae, *Switzerland–Example of Cultural
Coexistence* (1964).
[38] Speech by Senator Edmund S. Muskie, in the U.S. Senate, March 25, 1966,
"The Challenge of Creative Federalism."

ernment, it becomes clear that the restrictive, or rather restraining, features of classical federalism are being maintained and that creative federalism therefore depends upon an even more advanced sophistication concerning the operation of federalism as a process. The prospect of its being successfully operated in developing countries is feeble indeed.

There was fairly widespread optimism both inside and outside Nigeria that this largest African state might possibly prove the exception to the general trend toward centralization and authoritarianism.[39] To be sure, there were more skeptical voices.[40] One author noted "a certain stiffening of attitude" of the governing party toward all opposition elements; these tendencies have since led to a revolutionary upheaval and the suspension of the Constitution, including its federal features. It is only the latest in a series of such overthrows of artificial constitutional regimes which were created by the hidden impulse of a foreign (colonial) constituent power working through small groups of converts to Western constitutionalism.[41]

XI – *The Development of Politics*

Reviewing the reflections presented in the preceding pages in the light of the sketched data and brief hunches as to trends, the reader cannot help but feel somewhat bewildered. A similar impression results from the many and often brilliant efforts at comprehension of a very maelstrom of chaotic changes. Is not the very term *development* a euphemism, a Western gloss upon a world in utter tur-

[39] Taylor Cole, "Emergent Federalism" in *The Nigerian Political Scene*, Robert O. Tilman and Taylor Cole, eds. (1962), p. 47, reports a Nigerian paper as saying: "We chose the Federal System of Government because we realized that this is the only way to keep the diverse elements together." Cole, accepting the federalism-as-process conception, suggests that "federalism is the process by which adjustment is made between those forces making for disunity and those making for unity." But he did not commit himself as to which would prevail in Nigeria.

[40] Henry Bretton, *Power and Stability in Nigeria: The Politics of Decolonization* (1962); see also his "Political Influence in Southern Nigeria," in Herbert J. Spiro, ed., *Africa: The Primacy of Politics* (1966), pp. 49ff.

[41] See Ralph Braibanti and Joseph J. Spengler, eds., *Tradition, Values, and Socio-Economic Development* (1961), especially the essay by Joseph J. Spengler, "Theory, Ideology, Non-Economic Values, and Politico-Economic Development," in which a useful definition of *development* in general is offered on p. 8, and quoted in this essay, below.

moil? Before concluding, it may be well to take up once more this basic consideration. At the outset the term *development* was primarily and perhaps even basically a term related to the economy, its planning and administration. As one very broad definition puts it: "Development in general takes place when an index of that which is deemed desirable and relatively preferable increases in magnitude." [42] It is usually related to "modernization," which has been spoken of as entailing "the replacement of sacred revelation and revealed codes by secular enlightenment in respect of guidance in human affairs." [43] These characterizations leave a wide margin of uncertainty even in economic and technical matters. When it comes to politics, who is to say what is "desirable" and what "relatively preferable"? Is not the entire "great game of politics" played with a view to determining what is the answer to such questions as these? There is real danger here that one moves in a perfect circle of argumentation. An interesting illustration is provided by the subfield of administration.[44] It is often noted that "economic development has been blocked to a large extent precisely because its implementation depends on a structure and disposition of bureaucracy, neither of which can be jarred out of the larger societal whole." [45] Since that is very true, it is implied that the entire society's change is to be directed in terms of economic goals, the relative weight of which in the total scale of the given society's value system is precisely the issue. The recommendations which are offered as clearly rational, if administrative efficiency is desired, are taken from the Western experience in which the modern bureaucratic organization and its twin, the capitalistic economy, are embedded.[46]

Development, then, is not merely something "economic," nor are "economists" (specialists in the broadly defined sphere of economic factors) necessarily the only experts to be consulted on development.

[42] Spengler, *op. cit.*, p. 8.

[43] Daniel Lerner, *The Passing of Traditional Society* (1958), pp. 43f.

[44] Intrinsically careful studies are W. D. Reeve, *Public Administration in Siam* (1951); Sir Charles Collins, *Public Administration in Ceylon* (1951); Ralph Braibanti and Joseph J. Spengler, eds., *Administration and Economic Development in India* (1963).

[45] Braibanti and Spengler, eds., *op. cit.*, p. v.

[46] For a recent striking illustration see the report *Development Administration in Malaysia* by John D. Montgomery and Milton J. Esman (Kuala Lumpur: 1966). There on p. vi the accurate observation is made that *development administration* means at once development of administration and administration of development.

There exists a tendency to speak of all factors other than the economic as noneconomic factors. Such a way of discussing developmental problems implies that these problems are essentially economic, with cultural and political factors operating as "interferences." The political dimension is, however, *sui generis* and constitutes a distinct variable to which the political leadership of developing countries is particularly sensitive. Aware of the distinctive nature of the political community which they rule, its characteristic values, interests, and beliefs, these leaders often underestimate the contribution that a truly general political science has to make to the solution of their problems. Even so, in matters of culture and politics underdevelopment is a questionable proposition at best. Some of the countries standing in most pressing need of development, like India and the nations of Latin America, are the homes of highly advanced cultures, with a complex tradition of politics. While it may be very true, as Herbert J. Spiro has argued, that there should be a greater attention given to the "development of politics" in these emergent countries, as contrasted with the "politics of development," it is necessary to bear in mind that "politics" is an ancient craft in India and elsewhere. Anyone who has some time studied the Arthashastra—misnamed the Indian Machiavelli—will agree that sophistication in matters political had advanced as far in India at the time of Aristotle as it had in the West.[47] It was, however, in contrast to Aristotle's science of the *polis,* understood as the science of kingship (rulership). But such a science can become very elaborate and sophisticated, as the development of mercantilism and cameralism in the absolute monarchy in Europe clearly show. So unless we base the term's meaning upon the Western pattern of development from absolutism to constitutionalism, it remains an open question just what the "development of politics" in the sense of political development means.

The case of the Soviet Union shows—as did the absolute monarchies of the seventeenth and eighteenth centuries—that the needs of economic and industrial development can be met with considerable success by autocratic regimes. Sociological theories about ra-

[47] Charles Drekmeyer, *Kingship and Community in Ancient India* (1962), has gone much further back, but his discussion of the Arthashastra in Chapts. XI and XII illustrates our point well. He writes, correctly I believe, that "Kautalya goes far beyond Machiavelli in his attention to the structure and processes of administration" (p. 209). The date of the Arthashastra is controversial, but the earlier is preferable.

tionality as a standard and its development in the West and related notions about the legality of procedures in strictly Western terms have obscured this obvious fact and have given rise to hopes that the progress of industrialization would bring with it, if not democratization, then at least constitutionalism. The actual progress of development in the Soviet Union and elsewhere has belied these expectations. But the difficulty in adopting the Soviet model is actually as great, if not greater, than that of following the Western example.[48] Communism too presupposes the Western heritage, in some ways more completely even than Western modes of political conduct. Its extremes of rationalism and rule-begotten legalism are inconceivable without the context of Marx's radical acceptance and elaboration of the technology of industrial advance and its ethical antecedents.

If, then, neither the Soviet Union nor the West have any ready-made model to fit the needs of developing countries, is there no ground upon which to propose a rational model? Does the experience of mankind in politics fail to provide worthwhile insights by which to be guided in organizing the newly emergent nations? Many say: no. But I believe that an affirmative answer ought to be attempted. Such an answer may comprise merely a paradigmatic design, but, like a good map, it helps in basic orientation.[49] It may also be cast in terms of policy recommendations, or guidelines. These do not necessarily constitute a fully developed model, but they imply one. Such guidelines embody, of course, value judgments, especially in negative terms.[50] In any case, the term *political*

[48] This point is developed at greater length in a recent volume by Carl J. Friedrich and Zbigniew Brzezinski, *Totalitarian Dictatorship and Autocracy*, 2nd ed. (1965), Chaps. 2 and 28. See also Kurt London, ed., *New Nations in a Divided World* (1963), especially Part III, papers by David T. Cattell, "The Soviet Union Seeks a Policy for Afro-Asia" (pp. 163-79), Sergius Jakobson, "The U.S.S.R. and Ethiopia: A Case of Traditional Behavior" (pp. 180-92), and William E. Griffith, "Communist Polycentrism and the Underdeveloped Areas" (pp. 274-86). These problems also constitute a major theme in my *Man and His Government*.

[49] I have sketched such a model in my recent work, *Man and His Government* (1963), Chap. XXXV. To those who would argue that such a general model is of small practical use, since each emergent country presents very specific problems, I would reply that I entirely agree, but we need both a measuring rod and a series of guideposts. Economists, when speaking of economic development, likewise operate with a notion of a model economic order.

[50] They were suggested by Herbert J. Spiro, in *Government by Constitution— The Political Systems of Democracy* (1959), who would speak of "ideologism"

development when used in either the sense of the "politics of development" or of the "development of politics"—and perhaps especially when in both senses, because of their close relationships—presupposes a "vision" of the goal or goals, a fairly definite sense of what would be the "desirable" or the "relatively preferable." American go-getters once were proud "not to know where we're going, but merely that we're on the way." They sensed it very well; their notions of progress were in their very instincts. Such a naïve and unproblematic sense is no longer ours.

XII – Conclusion

It is, to conclude, the sum of these reflections that *tout ça change, tout c'est la même chose*. The new countries need governments that will function effectively in solving their problems by suitable public policies. These governments ought to be constitutional, but cannot be, because the prerequisites of constitutional government are lacking and will have to be developed. This is a slow process involving all the basic tasks which general political theory has identified. Its teachings are neglected at their peril by both practitioners and analysts of government in newly developing countries. There is little sense in insisting that the only yardstick is government in Britain or in the United States—as if one thought that all was working satisfactorily here—but there is equally little sense in treating the "new world" as so new that no past political and constitutional experience applies to its operations. The middle road is, as so often in life, the one which men with their limited means will be well advised to travel both in theory and practice. It means that we heed the dictum that "to govern is to invent," a favorite saying of one of the most successful political leaders in the field of development. Innovation is the means to lasting success, and not only in the emergent countries.

and "legalism"; though the negative consequences of both phenomena are admitted, it is not easy to see how they could be avoided. Hence some of the guidelines smack somewhat of utopian counsels of perfection.

II

Nationalism in a New Perspective: The African Case

Ibrahim Abu-Lughod

I – The Early Elusiveness of African Nationalism

Lord Hailey's incredibly rich survey of the African continent, conceived and successfully executed in the mid-thirties in order to summarize "the state of our knowledge regarding the problems . . . involved in the development of Africa; . . . to describe the physical and social background out of which these problems have arisen, and to analyze the factors which . . . must determine their solution," [1] managed to accomplish its admirable task without ever alluding to any public pressures for change generated by Africans or their national organizations. A contemporary reader would have assumed that the movement to liberalize government in Africa and to guide the gradual transition to the "national self-government" envisaged for Africa was to a large extent dependent upon the liberal conscience of imperial governments. He would have assumed that the chief problems involved in making the transition to self-government were those related to reconciling a divided public in the home countries and to gaining the acceptance of the European settlers on the African continent. Nowhere in that weighty volume

IBRAHIM ABU-LUGHOD is Associate Professor of Government at Smith College and spent the year 1965-66 as visiting professor at the Institute of Islamic Studies of McGill University. He is the author of *The Arab Rediscovery of Europe: A Study in Cultural Encounters* and is a frequent contributor to professional journals.

[1] Lord Hailey, *An African Survey: A Study of Problems Arising in Africa South of the Sahara* (London: Oxford University Press, 1938, 1945), p. xxi.

did Lord Hailey raise the question of African nationalism and its expression, nor did he suggest that it constituted an important stimulus to the reappraisals and reformulations taking place.

The enormous prestige of this authoritative work may perhaps have influenced another study which appeared shortly thereafter under the sponsorship of the same Royal Institute of International Affairs. Certainly the anonymous authors of *Nationalism*,[2] commissioned on the eve of World War II to survey the growth and pressures of nationalism and nationalist movements, presumably throughout the world, managed also to accomplish their assigned task without mentioning any indigenous movement of African nationalism, either north or south of the Sahara. Significantly, the only nationalism within Africa of which they took even slight cognizance was Afrikaaner nationalism.

These studies may well reflect the blind spots of the period. The European image of Africa was still a condescending one, and the British observers may have reassured themselves that the endemic diseases which in Europe, the Americas, and Asia had given rise to the malignancy of nationalism were not likely to occur there. It was perhaps assumed that these diseases find their most fertile soil in areas with a long history of civilized existence. Perhaps, then, Africa had a natural immunity to protect it from the contaminations of nationalist movements. Furthermore, since the authors were concerned with the effects of nationalist movements upon the stability of the world system, they apparently saw no African movement with potential to affect that stability.

Less than a generation later the major part of the African continent was independent and had already become an active and sometimes disturbing component of the world system. The number of independent African states will undoubtedly be augmented in the future by those still in the process of achieving their independence, whether peacefully or violently. It would be an interesting exercise if we could ask these authors of the '30s to account for what certainly appears to be an unusual phenomenon. Can these African states really have attained their independent status without inventing their own type of nationalism?

There is no doubt that, despite all the reservations one encounters in the literature concerning the preconditions for the growth and

[2] Royal Institute of International Affairs, *Nationalism* (London: Oxford University Press, 1939). It is to be noted that by then there had been no less than four Pan-African Congresses.

maturation of nationalism,[3] Africans did evolve a high degree of national consciousness which in the course of history was translated into concrete political movements in search of independence and sovereignty. And to a large extent the immediate aspirations of that consciousness have been fulfilled. The realization of complementary aspirations is still one of the unfinished tasks of African nationalism, but we may note that the public policies of the more influential African states are designed to add substance to symbolic sovereignty.

We can thus dismiss the idea that independence arrived *in vacuo* and can proceed to examine the alternative explanation, namely, that nationalism in Africa was present in a somewhat unique form. The Royal Institute authors, as well as Lord Hailey with his Indian experience, accustomed to employing certain categories and equipped with certain tools, did not comprehend the worldwide nature of the phenomenon. Not only were their tools defective, but the new manifestations were sufficiently different so as to elude their perceptions. They, like most students of nationalism, were familiar with its European, American, and Asian forms. While each of these had distinguishing qualities and attributes arising out of specific historic and societal experiences, they had more in common with one another than with the African variety of nationalism. Chronologically, African nationalism in its political form is the youngest, which gives it not only special qualities but also some significant advantages. For one thing, it was able to benefit from the collective experience of other nationalisms. For another, it benefited from the nature of the much altered world in which it achieved its maturity and fulfillment.

I suggest that African nationalism, then, is sufficiently different to justify its treatment apart from the analysis accorded to more conventional types of European and Asian nationalism. African nationalism's unique qualities stem from multiple factors, the nature and meaning of which will be explored in this chapter. Perhaps five basic factors may be singled out. First, the secular nature of the *milieu* in which African nationalism grew. Second, the changed philosophical climate in which the ideology of African

[3] The literature on nationalism is replete with these reservations, especially when authors try to define *nationalism* and find certain "essential" elements for its growth lacking. For a review of these and other interesting points see Louis Snyder, *The Meaning of Nationalism* (New Brunswick, N.J.: Rutgers University Press, 1954), and Boyd C. Shafer, *Nationalism: Myth and Reality* (New York: Harcourt, Brace & World, Inc. 1955).

nationalism was nurtured. Third, the type of leadership that chan-
neled its energies. Fourth, its peculiar symbiosis with the "emancipation" movements of the New World. Finally, the altered significance of the concept of sovereignty as an organizing principle of
the modern state. In combination, these elements gave rise to a
phenomenon that must be comprehended on its own terms, apart
from the more general propositions of nationalism. To do otherwise, as has thus far been done by students of Afro-Asian nationalism,[4] is to obscure the important issues involved.

II – The Secular Milieu

The independent nation-states of the world today were formed
within and grew out of the major civilizations that man created.
Accepting Toynbee's classification, all the major civilizations of
mankind have been predominantly religious in nature, being based
upon a distinctive theocentric system and having laws and norms
to guide man's actions, to regulate his conduct and his relations to
fellow men and to society, elaborated and codified in specific texts.
The five major civilizations identified by Toynbee—the Far Eastern, the Hindu, the Islamic, and the two Christian ones—account
for today's independent Euro-American and Asian states as well as
those portions of Africa that came under the Islamic influence.[5]
There was no room in Toynbee's *Study* for a specifically African
civilization. To that extent, African states, from their inception,
apparently managed to grow without the religious background.
This has had very serious implications for the development of na-

[4] The most comprehensive attempt so far is that of Rupert Emerson's *From
Empire to Nation: The Rise to Self-Assertion of Asian and African Peoples*
(Boston: Beacon Press, 1962). Valuable as that work is, it does not succeed in
projecting the uniquely African qualities of nationalism.

[5] Here we might digress slightly to ascertain the place of North Africa within
our discussion. Accepting Toynbee's scheme, North Africa's independent states
have more in common with their Asian counterparts than with their sub-
Saharan neighbors. The fundamental belief system, the specific problems faced
by nascent North African nationalism, and the ideological underpinnings of
that nationalism were basically Arab-Islamic in nature. The development of
political institutions and the visions of the future which the articulate North
African leadership conceived were, again, Arab-Islamic, as modified by modernity. Their strategy and tactics demanded a closer involvement with their
Arab neighbors than with their sub-Saharan ones. Because of these factors, we
will exclude North Africa from our discussion and focus chiefly upon sub-
Saharan Africa.

tional consciousness and for the political systems which emerged as a result.

The emergence of the European states out of a medieval Christian background is too familiar to require further elaboration. The rise of the Asian states does not differ radically, and in many instances the problems they experienced duplicated those of the earlier prototype, even though the context was slightly different. Both European and Asian developments of national consciousness shared basically similar conditions which determined the shape of polity and the resulting problems. Their absence from the African *milieu* gives African nationalism its first significant element of uniqueness.

The first manifestations of national consciousness and, therefore, the early attempts of the European and Asian civilizations to translate that consciousness into concrete political reality in the form of national states meant, *inter alia,* a rejection of the original premises of the religiously rooted political system, religiously defined political frontiers, and the religiously based membership in the political community. It will be recalled that in the European medieval setting, as in the later Asian setting, membership in the political community was reckoned in terms of faith. Thus Christians, Muslims, Hindus, Buddhists, and Confucians were all members of specific communities whose frontiers corresponded more or less to the preponderance of the faithful within a given territory. Members of such groups already had in common a set of beliefs about the world, about nature, and about themselves, beliefs that stemmed from their religious heritage. In other words, they already had in common a program and an ideology. Furthermore, while the governing of men and society was still accomplished by coercion and sheer power, its claim for legitimacy was derived from a supernatural source. When these premises were challenged under the influence of various events, substitute doctrines emerged for which adherents were sought and in the name of which the frontiers of the state had to be redrawn. In both Europe and Asia this implied the emergence of secularism in its broadest sense: secularism in terms of thought and ideology, secularism in terms of politics and society, and secularism in terms of culture.

We find in examining the Asian example that to a large extent it paralleled the European. The first manifestations of national consciousness in Asia—China, India, the Near East—assumed a religious form or had to contend with religious norms. Assaulted and perhaps even conquered by the European who was of a different faith, Asian leaders tried to mobilize the masses to counteraction in the name of their own faith. The earliest efforts of Asian leaders to achieve a regeneration in culture and society sufficient to free themselves from European dominance were directed to the reform of religious institutions. This may have been natural, for in the eighteenth and the nineteenth centuries Asian patterns of thought and the Asian *Weltanschauung* were essentially medieval in character, relatively untouched by the forces of modernity. But there were other reasons as well. The Asian leaders were trying to mobilize the masses, and to do so effectively they had to appeal to meaningful cultural symbols which were still religious in nature. Furthermore, the bond uniting members of the community was religion. For these reasons nationalism in its first Asian manifestation was religious in form and content.[6]

With time, however, Asian leadership underwent change and in the process discovered that the older norms were insufficient to mobilize people to action. National aspirations expressed within the framework of a religious system proved inadequate to achieve a meaningful dialogue with the European ruler whose consent for the attainment of autonomy and independence gradually became more important. Realizing these limitations, Asian leaders sought a substitute principle of attraction, one which could both achieve the desired national cohesion and be acceptable to the European ruler. Thus there was a transition from the religious to the ethnic-linguistic and territorial types of nationalism.

Both types of nationalism had to overcome older loyalties, and which of the two ultimately became a rallying point for a particular nationalist ideology depended in large measure upon the specific characteristics of each culture area. In general, where society was composed of heterogeneous linguistic and/or ethnic groups or, alternately, where the territory had well defined and relatively stable

---

[6] The intimate connection between nationalism and religion, especially in the West, is sensitively depicted in Salo Baron, *Modern Nationalism and Religion* (New York: Harper & Row, Publishers, 1947). Practically all studies of Asian nationalism bear this out; see for various illustrations the following "national" studies: K. M. Pannikkar, *Asia and Western Dominance* (London: George Allen & Unwin, 1953); George M. Kahin, *Nationalism and Revolution in Indonesia* (Ithaca, N.Y.: Cornell University Press, 1953), pp. 37-63; Albert Hourani, *Arabic Thought in the Liberal Age* (London: Oxford University Press, 1962); Charles Heimsath, *Indian Nationalism and Hindu Social Reform* (Princeton: Princeton University Press, 1964); and Niyazi Berkes, *The Development of Secularism in Turkey* (Montreal: McGill University Press, 1964).

frontiers, territorial nationalism with its emphasis upon the *patrie* emerged as the dominant ideology. The Indian, the Egyptian, and to some extent the Chinese cases are good examples of this type of nationalism in Asia. On the other hand, where inhabitants spoke a common language and believed in a specific ethnic identity and perhaps some common ancestral heritage, emphasis on ethnic-linguistic principles of nationalism prevailed. The Arab and Turkish cases are good illustrations of this type.

Regardless of which type ultimately emerged, however, the new nationalisms redefined membership in the political community and reformulated the principle of authority and the source of its legitimacy. For the wider community of "believers," for a supernatural source of political authority, and for the operation of a religiously based system of law and ethics were substituted secular bonds which began to claim the allegiance of the community. Thus, instead of Muslims, Hindus, and Buddhists, reference began to be made to Arabs, Turks, Indians, Burmese, and Chinese. These identities, while applied ambiguously at times, became meaningful nevertheless, not only to the people themselves but to the outside world as well. In a similar fashion "mandates from the people," man-made law, and a humanistic belief system began to replace the older principles of legitimacy and control. As students of contemporary history and politics, we cannot but be fully aware that the transition was neither simple nor painless. The religious past constitutes a heavy legacy from which the present states of Asia must continue to extricate themselves.

A second characteristic shared by the nationalisms developed in Europe and Asia is their exclusiveness. Whether the bonds of membership and community cohesion are religious, ethnic-linguistic, or territorial, they still imply an exclusion of those who fail to share the bond. Since nowhere in the world today are there totally homogeneous populations, national polity based upon religion (for example, Pakistan and Israel) creates a minority and excluded status for some, as does the polity based upon ethnic or linguistic identity. In modern times we expect responsible states to guarantee full rights to all citizens, but we are all too painfully aware of the travail of minorities everywhere and of the tensions involved in majority-minority relations. Even the territorial basis of nationalism is not free from exclusivity, for to view all those on the wrong side of the border as antagonists places obstacles in the way of wider unities.

By contrast, the African case reveals certain features peculiarly its own. Relatively free from a competing indigenous religious past (again, excepting the Islamic areas and Ethiopia), Africans on the whole had an easier time in evolving national consciousness completely free from the religious coloration and the conflicts that accompanied it elsewhere. Not only this, but they were free to develop whichever secular bonds seemed most suitable and to advance patterns of thought and ideology which were, in the first instance, humanistically oriented. It is therefore not surprising that the intellectual content of their nationalist programs was decidedly different, and their social and political problems of organization at least somewhat different, from those confronted elsewhere. And to that extent we can predict that development in Africa not only is but undoubtedly will continue on a different path.

The most striking aspect of national consciousness in Africa is its continental territorial perspective. Lacking the ready-made bond of a universal religion and confronted with multiple and sometimes conflicting ethnic and linguistic groups, it was natural for African leaders to articulate their aspirations for independence and liberty in territorial terms. But by *territory* they did not mean merely the areas whose boundaries had been defined by the occupying powers. The African leaders who struggled for independence, while doing so within specific areas under the jurisdiction of one or another major European power, nevertheless demanded independence in terms of Africa as a whole. There was a definite feeling of African-ism present,[7] which dictated a special concept of territory: not the Gold Coast or Tanzania or Senegal, but Africa. And when the movements for African independence gained momentum and became more political, Africans throughout the continent were called upon to participate not necessarily in the name of their particular territory—although that was the immediate target—but in the name of Africa.

The implicit demand for loyalty to the continent was consciously defined by African leaders. The various Pan-African Congresses held in Europe, and later in Africa, conceived of independence for the whole, and rarely was much attention paid to the narrowly

[7] Whether this Africanism was born out of conflict, positive elements, or the capricious whims of map-makers, though very significant, is not central to our inquiry. For an excellent discussion of the "brotherhood" thus created see Ali Mazrui, "On the Concept 'We are All Africans'," in the *American Political Science Review* LVII, No. 1 (1963), 88-97.

defined territorial entities that sent delegates to these Congresses. Later, when African political parties emerged and assumed responsibility for mobilizing and organizing the masses for political action, they frequently assumed the label *African* rather than labels implying a smaller territorial base. While each of these parties pressed for immediate independence of the particular territory in which it operated, this was viewed merely as a tactic of expediency. The ultimate aspiration of the more significant political parties was independence for all of Africa. It was not accidental, therefore, that African leaders, soon after the attainment of independence, sought to organize a union of African states. They were, by experience and moral imperatives, committed to that task. Their seeming inability to bring about a functionally effective union at present does not invalidate the depth of their aspiration.

Furthermore, and again in sharp contrast to the demands and strategies of Asian nationalisms, independence for Africa, from the perspective of its leaders, was indivisible. So long as some segment of Africa remained unfree, the African sense of achievement was incomplete and the African sense of dignity still unassuaged. At no point did any of the Asian nationalisms identify themselves so completely and so personally with each other's aspirations, nor did they view the struggles of each as part of their own. While sympathetic to one another because of common experience with imperialism, their sympathies rarely transcended verbal or moral support. By contrast, African support of and assistance to less fortunate parts of the continent has been material and concrete. After all, the struggle is one and so is the achievement.

Thus African nationalism developed along more comprehensive lines than had earlier types; it became a more inclusive movement than any of the Asian varieties. It conceived of the inhabitants of Africa as brothers, a concept which dictated a corresponding political strategy and organization. Because of this concept Africa's leadership found room for those who might not otherwise be considered within their purview. We may cite Black Africa's support of North African independence and its willingness, after the attainment of independence by all, to incorporate North Africa within the African context. It will be recalled that North Africa's nationalism developed first and fought its battles for independence and articulated its aspirations much earlier. And yet, during that entire period the leaders of North Africa hardly took cognizance of the travail of their southern neighbors. While their behavior is understandable in terms of their cultural background and history, further explanation is found in the exclusive nature of North Africa's nationalism. By contrast, Black Africa exhibited immediate concern for North Africa's ordeal and gave early support to its claim for independence.[8] Despite some dissension within African ranks[9] the view that Africa was One, regardless of the past, prevailed. Whether the same spirit of inclusiveness will govern the behavior of Africans towards racially and ethnically different minorities within the confines of the continent itself—as yet unclear—will constitute an important test of how sharply the qualities of African nationalism contrast with those of other nationalisms.

III – Climate for the Ideology

The absence of an overpowering religious system in African nationalism meant not only that the territorial principle could be flexibly followed but also that Africa's leadership was free to evolve its programs and ideas about the state and society out of existing systems of thought, guided only by the limiting factors of the African *milieu*. This meant that Africa's traditions could be reconciled with the most advanced patterns of thought current in the modern world. By the time African nationalism arrived upon the scene, the intellectual climate of the world was heavily impregnated with socialist principles and visions of society—a far cry from the climate of thought that had confronted earlier nationalisms.

Asian nationalist reformers had to reconcile their religious past with the liberal ideology of nineteenth-century Europe; the conflict between the two was in part epistemological, and in the difficult reconciliation much intellectual energy was expended. But Africa's leadership could deal with the existing problems of society and culture, taking for granted the superiority of rationality and

[8] It will be recalled that Dr. Du Bois wished to convene the Fourth Pan-African Congress (1927) on African soil and his choice fell upon Tunis. His wish was frustrated by the French authorities then occupying Tunisia. The Fifth Pan-African Congress (1945) openly supported the demands of North Africans for independence. See George Padmore, *Pan-Africanism or Communism* (London: Dennis Dobson, 1956), p. 168, for text.

[9] The few Africans who openly dissented are not in the mainstream of African thought; Chief Awolowo, leader of a splinter and parochial movement within Nigeria opposed the admission of North Africans into the African Concert, and so did Moise Tshombe. See Colin Legum, *Pan-Africanism* (London: Pall Mall Press, 1962), pp. 66, 266-71.

the validity of the scientific approach to human existence. Only a discredited magic stood in the way. Furthermore, instead of deriving their social and economic principles from liberalism—the dominant pattern of political thought evolved by the nation-states of Europe and received by the Asian nationalists in the late nineteenth and early twentieth centuries—African nationalist leaders had already witnessed the shortcomings of liberalism and of its successful challengers. They opted for the more advanced patterns of socialism, which, in their construction, turned out to be more in harmony with African cultural patterns than liberalism would have been.

The influence of these two types of ideology and the different traditional pasts of Asian and African societies had significant implications for the development of society and politics in both places. In the Asian case the acceptance of liberalism meant that a transition had to be made to secularism, and this transition is still far from being accomplished successfully anywhere.[10] In its early and accepted form secularism meant, among other things, that religion and the state ought to be kept separate, with each functioning on different levels and for different ultimate purposes. It was believed that the interests of each would be enhanced by separation. On the social and economic level liberalism posed even more perplexing problems. Liberalism, of course, had postulated the principle of government abstention from active intervention in the social and economic order. While protective principles adopted by the community were to be implemented by government, it was not considered the legitimate function of government to enforce

[10] The literature on modern Asian politics is replete with references to the problems of religion and politics. A question which is increasingly being posed, in the light of the religious background of all Asian states, is whether the secular state is possible at all. See for example D. E. Smith's study *India as a Secular State* (Princeton: Princeton University Press, 1963), in which he depicts the difficult path of secularism in India, or Ved Prakash Luthera, *The Concept of the Secular State and India* (Bombay: Oxford University Press, 1964), in which the Indian author asserts the relative impossibility of establishing a secular state within the present framework of Hindu India. For similar questions, but affecting Islamic areas, see Ibrahim Abu-Lughod, "The Islamic Factor in African Politics," *ORBIS*, VIII, No. 2 (Summer 1964), 425-44 and "Retreat from the Secular Path?: Islamic Dilemmas of Arab Politics," *The Review of Politics*, XXVIII, No. 4 (October 1966), 447-76. The March 1965 issue of the Indian periodical *Seminar* (New Delhi) is devoted to the implications of secularism and contains an excellent bibliography (pp. 51-53) on the problems of religion and politics throughout the world; significantly, few references deal with Africa.

norms and doctrines beyond those that might emerge from the normal and unfettered operation of natural economic laws. As a result, Asian leaders pressing the cause of independence rarely gave any indication of the type of social and economic systems that ought to prevail after independence. Their objective was merely to wrest control of the machinery of government and return it to native hands. Thus, when they did obtain independence and as-sume the reins of government, Asian leaders were immediately con-fronted with serious difficulties which claimed the lives of some of them and ultimately shook these new states to their founda-tions.[11] The old laissez-faire principle of liberalism which had guided their political agitation for so long could not, in fact, meet the needs of contemporary independent nation-states. Once this vacuum was recognized, there was an attempt to make the transi-tion to some type of socialist system, a process now very much in evidence throughout Asia.

African leaders, whose religious background, when present, was derivative in nature, had grown in an atmosphere of almost total acceptance of secular society; for the most part there was no con-flict on this issue when the independent state emerged.[12] But they also functioned in an atmosphere of socialist principles and prac-tices which by the thirties was quite advanced in Europe and by the forties had already triumphed. The African leaders, whether members of the educated elite awaiting their opportunity in some European capital or engaged in the struggle locally as representa-tives of some functional group, had absorbed that ideology.[13] Even before independence was attained, their programs of agitation had already delineated the type of political and social organization

[11] The Indian Congress is one exception; it managed to make the intellectual transition to socialism during the period of the struggle for independence. The Chinese Communists provide another exception, but their opponents have much in common with the rest of that generation of Asian nationalists.

[12] Again Islamic areas and Ethiopia are exceptional and point out the affinity which these have with Asian nationalisms.

[13] Though African thought has been eclectic, the socialist component in that eclecticism is quite apparent in the writings of African nationalists and the programs they tried to carry out in the post-independence period. See Thomas Hodgkin, "A Note on the Language of African Nationalism," in K. Kirkwood, ed., St. Anthony's Papers, No. 10, African Affairs (London: Chatto & Windus, Ltd., 1961), pp. 22-40; William H. Friedland and Carl G. Rosberg, eds., African Socialism (Stanford: Stanford University Press, 1964); and L. S. Senghor, On African Socialism, trans. Mercer Cook (New York: Frederick A. Praeger, Inc., 1964).

of society that was to emerge afterwards. We know from their many pronouncements and polemics that some variety of socialist state was envisaged. Their early commitment to individual liberty was joined with an absolute commitment to an egalitarian society, possibly in the context of socialism, in which government was to play an active and dynamic role.

While these commitments may be attributed to the intellectual climate in which socialist patterns of thought were coming to prevail, this does not constitute the sole explanation. Other and equally significant factors played a part. The presence of these factors (discussed in the next section) in the African context and their relative absence in the Asian setting help to explain the divergent routes followed by the two sets of leadership in setting a political course.

IV – The Origins of Leadership

Of perhaps basic importance is the fact that the type of leadership that dominated the African scene differed significantly from that of the Asian in terms of origins, socio-economic background, and class affinity. This could not help but lead them into different solutions. It is readily observed that the African leaders, on the whole, came from the small, urbanized, Western-educated groups with only minimal and tenuous connections to the traditional classes of leadership. It will be recalled that the Europeans, once in total control of the African territories, evolved policies calculated to win over the defeated elites. These policies, slightly obscured by the oft repeated but misleading distinction between the "direct" and "indirect" patterns of administration followed by France and Great Britain, had the effect of identifying the interests and aspirations of the occupying powers with those of the chiefs, emirs, and other traditional leaders.

A challenge to the occupation, then, meant *ipso facto* a challenge to the rule of the traditional class, and vice versa. As a result, when the challenge ultimately did materialize, it came from those elements of society most removed from the actual or spiritual jurisdiction of traditional groups and from those elements most capable of using a successful blend of traditional and modern methods to attain their ends. Although the young leaders tried on occasion to enlist the support of the traditional chiefs, they were not dependent upon such collaboration for the achievement of their aims. The stage and foci of their operations were the complex and growing urban centers which increasingly drew into their orbits larger numbers of detribalized Africans whose loyalties and aspirations were developing along nontraditional lines.

Their methods of operation and the way they generated public pressure were again modern in nature. The complex network of professional organizations they developed, culminating in the emergence of political parties, were free from traditional control and the traditional wielders of that control.[14] Because of this independence African leaders were freer to evolve their ideological commitments on the basis of their own multiple intellectual and emotional affinities and to try to translate their ideologies into concrete public policies, regardless of the effects these might have upon the traditional organization of society and its class structure. In other words, they were not compelled to modify or dilute their programs in order to gain the support of traditional elements.

The national cohesion achieved in African areas was attained in the full light of the ideological commitments of the leadership, and those who supported the leadership knew in advance, though in varying degrees, the general direction the independent state would take. Additionally, and perhaps of equal importance, the African leaders themselves, while they had a vested interest in the future, had none in the existing social and economic order. Lacking a motivation for conserving their old status or interests, they were at greater liberty to move in directions more radical and principled than would have otherwise been the case. These may be the principal factors that account for the alacrity with which Africa's early leaders immersed themselves in the socialist vision of society then ascendant.

It is precisely the absence of these elements that, in addition to the ethos of liberalism which prevailed during their emergence, accounts for the relative failure of Asian nationalist leaders to develop a coherent set of principles to guide the future state. For

[14] Traditional parties and groupings, sometimes obstructing the process of liberation by their narrow perspectives or traditional methods (Mau Mau or Muslim groups in Nigeria and other areas), obviously coexisted with the more militant, comprehensive, doctrinaire parties. See Thomas Hodgkin, *African Political Parties*, (London: Penguin, 1961), and the more regional study of Ruth S. Morgenthau, *Political Parties in French-Speaking West Africa* (London: Oxford University Press, 1964). The various volumes edited by Gwendolen Carter contain valuable insights into the dynamics of party interaction with ideology and leadership.

it will be recalled that Asian nationalism, whether in its early or later stages, was the creation of multiple agents and elements of society.

The traditional upper classes of Asia, although defeated on the military and political level by the European occupation, continued to exercise a good measure of social and economic influence in society. They felt, furthermore, their loss of the levers of power much more keenly than their African counterparts. They had both a stake in the economic system and a grudge against it. They owned land, and they were concerned with their further economic —and consequently social and political—advancement. But the European elite, in control of the state machinery, gave free scope to European enterprises and European-protected ones, and a non-traditional and often nonindigenous upper social crust was gradually thrust up. The traditional classes agitated for better conditions within the occupation, but were most often unsuccessful, for European capitalism, then at its zenith, could not tolerate a competing native capitalist class. As a result, the traditional upper classes in various Asian societies countered by generating pressure on the occupation, pressure which, in the course of history, led to the emergence of the nationalist movement. Practically all the nationalist movements in Asia, in the beginning or later on, were led by the traditional elite, obviously transformed in the process of European occupation into a skilled and westernized elite.

In addition, the Asian nationalist movements drew into their orbits various other elements in society which had different and sometimes conflicting interests. The sole goal upon which these diverse elements could agree without revealing deep fissures in their ranks was the limited goal of independence. Had they tried to define more precisely the type of society to emerge after independence, undoubtedly the national unity they had achieved with such difficulty would have suffered grievously; hence the absence of concrete social and economic programs in Asian nationalist movements.

There is perhaps another factor that accounts for this absence. The traditional elite at the head of the nationalist movement was not seriously concerned with the public welfare of the masses. To this elite independence meant the resumption of their preeminent position in society, displacing the foreign usurpers. Serious consideration of radical change could not be countenanced.

Together, these elements in Asian nationalist leadership, sanctified perhaps by the prevalent European philosophy of liberalism,

explain the absence of concrete commitment to any type of social
and economic order other than one vaguely "liberal." The difficulties that have plagued the Asian states since their independence are
neither accidental nor incomprehensible. They are the logical consequences of the early doctrinal failure of Asian nationalism. And
it was only after those first trying years, during which the traditional
upper class was compelled to retreat from power, that an altogether
new type of leadership, having more in common with its African
counterpart, emerged to promulgate the socialist vision of society
with its attendant socialist apparatus for state planning and control.
African uniqueness may lie more in the skipping of the intermediate step than in the end result.

V – Symbiosis with Emancipation in the New World

The absence of religious background, maturation within the socialist environment of modern times, and leadership by nontraditional
elites still do not account for all of the differentiating qualities of
African nationalism. We must take into consideration the historic
evolution of the movement and the forces that played upon it.
While a comprehensive account is neither possible nor necessary
at this juncture of our inquiry, some broad indications of that
evolution are imperative to complete the picture.

Studies of African nationalism have thus far taken one or another
of two approaches. On the one hand, African nationalism has been
viewed as an internal movement arising out of self-assertion on the
part of indigenous Africans and utilizing all possible internal
forces for the attainment of its ends.[15] This approach predicates the
development of a specific type of consciousness which, while varying
from area to area, epitomizes the drive of all human groups, regardless of their ethnic, tribal, and linguistic identities, to rule
themselves. While this self-rule is often defined in narrow territorial
terms, that is, within the confines of specific areas whose frontiers
have been sufficiently hardened by administrative practice, occasionally we are told that there may be certain levels of consciousness in nationalism.[16] In either case, however, nationalism has

[15] Essentially this is Thomas Hodgkin's approach in *Nationalism in Colonial
Africa* (London: Frederick Muller, 1957).

[16] James S. Coleman, "Nationalism in Tropical Africa," in William J. Hanna,
ed., *Independent Black Africa* (Chicago: Rand McNally & Co., 1963). Valuable
from a slightly different perspective is Margery Perham's "The Psychology of
African Nationalism," *ibid.*, pp. 176-91.

been viewed as an internal response to European occupation, albeit deriving some of its principles and strategies from the outside and being influenced by external forces as well. To the extent that nationalism is viewed in this manner, African nationalism is simply a repetition, with only slight variations, of the Asian experience.

The other approach takes as its point of departure the emergence of a specific type of consciousness among Negroes during the "Diaspora." The strivings of the Negro for justice and equality in the New World are taken as the source of the rise of African nationalism and the movement for African independence. An intimate connection is predicated between these early post-emancipation movements seeking Negro rights and African regeneration on the one hand, and the climate of opinion surrounding Africa and ultimately the ideas of rising African leaders, on the other.[17] African leaders, trained in the United States and elsewhere, did find ready support and encouragement from these movements. In this respect the later development of African nationalism and its demands for a specific type of political independence are viewed as logical by-products of earlier manifestations in the New World.

While both of these views can be entertained and evidence amassed to support their validity, neither in fact is adequate to explain the nature and type of nationalism which ultimately prevailed in Africa. Both in some measure obscure certain fundamental issues in the development of African nationalism. In the absence of detailed studies of that development our own discussion must remain inconclusive. However, it is evident even on the basis of available accounts that there were in fact two streams of nationalist consciousness running parallel to each other, originating in different places in response to different pressures and emphasizing different needs and aspirations.

One, originating in the New World, sought to maximize the effective exercise of Negro rights guaranteed but not honored by the political system and, at the same time, to remove the stigma attached to their color which was seen as an obstacle hindering the enjoyment of these rights. To accomplish their ends, Negro leaders in the New World had to rehabilitate the image held by others of the African on the continent, to obtain for him and thus for themselves a more realistic appreciation from the world. In the final analysis, their interest in the welfare and development of Africa

---

[17] This is evident in the work of Padmore, *op. cit.*

stemmed from painful dilemmas within their own country. At the earliest stages they were not particularly concerned with the political aspects of African problems, nor were they involved in the issue of independence for Africa. Their concerns were more racial or cultural in nature, and out of this focus were to emerge the racial and cultural manifestations of African nationalism which, only later, merged with the preponderantly political strains of internal development. This external stream of nationalist consciousness was, in the form it assumed and the direction it followed, perhaps inevitable, but in no way could it have brought about the independence of Africa nor even have shaped the major premises of African nationalism.

The second stream of consciousness originated in Africa itself. While it had its own peculiar racial and cultural content, it was quite explicitly political in tone. It was articulate in its needs and aspirations and derived its support and strength from sources other than the earlier stream. At this stage of our knowledge we cannot yet state precisely when this second stream emerged, although the first can be pinpointed without much difficulty. However, we can at least be certain of one thing: we know that it could not have begun, full-blown, after the Second World War.[18]

Most discussions of African nationalism have assumed that the political direction of African nationalism was set by the Fifth Pan-African Congress in Manchester in 1945, which instructed the assembled African delegates to agitate in their home territories for the cause of independence. Presumably that was the time when African nationalism first assumed concrete political form and articulated political demands. We know that this could not have been the beginning. A movement does not emerge suddenly into the full light of history in that form. It must have had its antecedents and a history of past developments that made its supporters willing, at that particular place and time, to exert their pressures and to respond to the appeals of leadership.

Until more detailed studies of the origin of African nationalism appear,[19] we must leave this point and merely suggest that the 1945 date is significant for other reasons. It marks not the beginning of

[18] Hodgkin seems to suggest this in *Nationalism in Colonial Africa*, p. 10, as does L. G. Cowan, *The Dilemmas of African Independence* (New York: Walker & Co., 1964), p. 1.

[19] David Kimble, *A Political History of Ghana, 1850-1928* (Oxford: The Clarendon Press, 1963), is such a study.

a movement but the end of an earlier alliance. For up to then the two streams of consciousness were fuzzily merged, and in that merger the New World Negroes' needs and aspirations predominated, which accounts for the early emphasis upon racial and cultural aspects of nationalism.[20] Indigenous African nationalism had in a way to liberate itself from the cumulative effects and influences of the New World supporters if it was to achieve its politically and socially oriented goals. As it turned out, the needs and aspirations of the two communities were, in one way or another, quite different. The realization of their different yet symbiotic goals required operating within two very different contexts using different weapons. And so by 1945 the two streams parted company, each to assert itself in its original environment. Once this separation was accomplished, both movements gained, without, however, sacrificing those positive elements of their earlier cooperation.

Nor was either movement quite the same, for each had been broadened by the influence of the other during their alliance. Having been so affected by the racial and cultural aspects of Negro nationalism in the New World, African nationalism in the continental setting assumed a broader vision of itself as a unit shaped by many forces, including those of race and temperament. The racial emphasis, however, seems to have been rather mature and tolerant. There is nothing in the expressions of racial consciousness in contemporary African nationalism which would correspond to the arrogance of "Black Nationalists" in the U.S. For while the Africans may emphasize their racial qualities, they do not use them to defend their superiority. It is an emphasis born of acceptance and an implicit demand for recognition and equality. To that extent the egalitarian society which is demanded in Africa itself in social and economic terms is demanded also on a world level, but construed in racial terms. What this implies is an acceptance of a multiplicity of communities coexisting with equality.

Again we may note some significant contrasts with Asian nationalism. Asians, too, had suffered from racial discrimination at an early period, though perhaps not to the same extent. But whereas the travail of the Africans led them to oppose and condemn

---

[20] This merger is most evident in the work of Dr. Du Bois. A good summary of this symbiosis and some of its results can be found in St. Claire Drake, "Pan-Africanism, Negritude and the African Personality," in Hanna, *op. cit.*, pp. 530-41. See also G. Shepperson, "Notes on Negro American Influences on the Emergence of African Nationalism," *Journal of African History*, I, No. 2 (1960).

racial discrimination, no matter where it occurred, the Asians concerned themselves with this general issue only in the post-independence era. They had empathy neither with the problems of their fellow Asians nor with the more remote problems of the Africans. The worldwide movement against the color bar received substantial reinforcements from the Africans themselves. In this emphasis upon racial equality, first for Africans *vis à vis* others but also for all people, can be seen a reinforcement of certain universal, non-exclusive principles enunciated by Africans in their territorially based nationalism as well as their doctrinally guiding socialism.

There is yet one more basic historical element affecting the universal direction of African nationalism. Asians, in one form or another, had had statehood in the past. They had enjoyed fairly developed civilizations, and many of them had, exaggerated as it may have been in the expression of the nationalists, a "glorious" past. Almost all Asian nationalisms could invoke the symbol of this past, in which their position in the world had been more respectable, perhaps even preeminent. Thus, in their agitation for independence and dignity they were essentially trying to restore the "golden" past and to erase an interlude of debasement. Exclusivity was an implicit element in their approach.

African leaders, on the other hand, had greater difficulty in conjuring a past sufficiently glorious and tied closely enough to the specific territorial unit seeking its independence to inspire the masses. Rather than appealing to a symbolic past, they had to use the vision of creating a new civilization in the future. The result was that nationalism in Africa developed along futuristic and assertive lines and, because the symbols were independent of a specific historic and geographic referent, along fluid lines of potential universality. The absence of a golden era to be restored allowed the energies of African leaders to be directed toward the solution of present and future problems placed in a context wider than the confines of the territorially sovereign state.

VI – *The Transformation of Sovereignty*

The same difficulties which confronted Africa's leaders in conjuring an image of a glorious past lineally connected to the territorial state they happened to lead, however, also served the purpose of assisting them in their drive to articulate and realize a principle of political existence more viable than the "sovereign state." They could and in fact did identify themselves and the remainder of the continent with the achievements and contributions of earlier African groups which had occupied only portions of the territorial state.[21] It was perhaps natural for many African leaders, responding to the general denigration of their heritage by outsiders, to counter by alluding to the great classical civilizations of certain regions— Egypt, Ethiopia, Ghana, etc.—and by taking pride in their contributions to the world. It was difficult, however, to draw too close a connection between present-day Ghana and the ancient kingdom of that name or to link the African states too intimately with the Pharaonic civilization in the Nile Valley. The identification had to be phrased in broad terms. The leaders were thus required to view themselves in a wider context, namely, in the continental one, so that their present conditions could be traced legitimately to a significant past; this past became, then, a common one to be shared by all Africans.

This impulse, or indeed need, to stretch the historic identity to cover an entire continent was absent in Asia. The Indians, the Chinese, and the Arabs, to mention a few, could relate themselves much more easily to a specific territorial unit within which their particular glorious past had blossomed; there was no need, for nationalist purposes, to go beyond the more or less natural frontiers of the nation to seek that past. Consequently, the concept of a comprehensive, continental basis of identity has been totally absent in Asia.

In contrast with the Asian states, which have traditionally exhibited a high degree of attachment to and concern with the territorially sovereign state, the African states, regardless of their initial motives or reasons, have been far more willing to identify themselves with more distant territorial and temporal "relatives." This has led them to exhibit much less concern with the territorial state and its underlying idea of "sovereignty" for its own sake than many European and Asian nations. The doctrinal metamorphosis from "sovereignty as an end" to "sovereignty as a means" toward a higher form of political union has perhaps made smoothest progress in Africa.

It will be recalled that sovereignty was one of the important doctrines of international law and politics which characterized the early European nation-state system. Although initially an attribute

[21] Boutros Boutros-Ghali, "The Addis Ababa Charter—A Commentary," *International Conciliation,* No. 546 (Jan. 1964).

of the monarch, with the increasing acceptance of the nation as the basis of political existence sovereignty was attached by extension to the state, finally becoming the *sine qua non* of statehood. In its early legal and political formulation the doctrine implied that a territorial state, in order to be accepted as a viable and equal member of the international community, must possess the necessary authority and power to assert its jurisdiction within clearly defined frontiers, without dispute and subject to no limitations save those norms formulated in a mythical "natural law." In the course of the nineteenth and early twentieth centuries the doctrine of sovereignty and its corollary, the sovereign state, acquired such a degree of sacredness and universality that they were scarcely susceptible to any kind of theoretical or practical challenge.

The drive for independence by the Asian nationalists was launched in an atmosphere of universal acceptance of the validity of the doctrine of sovereignty. Their ambitions and aspirations were accordingly formulated in the light of both the assets and practical implications that full sovereignty entailed. For them, whether in the Far East, Southeast Asia, the Indian subcontinent, or Western Asia, the aim of the nationalist movement was to bring into existence a state, completely freed from any external disability which might curtail its unfettered internal control or prevent it from behaving with perfect freedom in the international arena. They were willing, like the European states which had inspired them, to accept only those obligations imposed by an imperfectly developed and imperfectly applied system of international law.

In the light of that struggle and its successful culmination in independent statehood the Asian states asserted their multiple rights and attachments to the doctrine of sovereignty and what it conferred on them in terms of international behavior. Their problem was to guard zealously the hard-won independence of the territorial state which they had attained, and they participated in international activities not only to protect those sovereign rights but to enhance them as well. It was not possible for them—intellectually, culturally, or otherwise—to advance a thesis which would contravene the validity of the sacred doctrine of sovereignty. They neither had the cultural foundations for a higher unity nor were they intellectually prepared at that time for an alternative formulation of the international system.

Yet, of course, the road was neither simple nor clear cut for many of these Asian states. Some of them had been split apart to form several states where in the past they had been one; others had been regrouped at the behest of certain powers or in response to specific forces and pressures. Where this occurred, the *status quo* was challenged, but the challenge did not necessarily reflect their defection from the ranks of the "sovereign righters." What they stated was simply this: Our nationalism, as we define it, has the aim of bringing about a political community encompassing all those members of the community sharing the unifying bond, whether of language, territory, or any other combination of factors. Since the present frontiers of the emancipated state still do not correspond to the "natural" frontiers, they should be revised. Thus, some of the Arab states, for example, have agitated for a broader unity to encompass all "natural" citizens, while Indonesia has "confronted" Malaysia over a similar issue. Irredentist movements the world over are, in part, a response to this initial disappointment of the nationalists.

Although they have endeavored to alter frontiers, the Asian states have not really deviated from the European doctrinal pattern. Their concern was and still is definitely national in scope. No regional regrouping of Asian states has been seriously envisaged, nor has any basic revision in the concept or meaning of sovereignty been attempted. Up to the present the Asian states have evidently not deemed it important or necessary to regroup themselves on more comprehensive grounds except for the inchoate purpose of influencing international politics. The Bandung Conference of 1955 and the subsequent conferences held by the nonaligned nations were manifestations of their desire to act collectively in order to exert pressure on the competing power spheres, without at the same time sacrificing or compromising any of the sovereign bases of their national existences.

The African leaders, however, were pursuing their nationalistic aspirations at a time when Europe itself was questioning and re-examining its own conceptions of the sovereign state. The defects of sovereignty and its ultimately destructive effects upon the world system, symbolized and made real by its almost total breakdown during two world wars, had given rise to competing conceptions of world order. Emphasis on sovereignty decreased perceptibly in the post-World War II period, and this decrease was reflected not only in the behavior of the states themselves but also in the work of international jurists and lawyers. A higher conception of world order was beginning to take hold. Instead of the old nation-state system, a transnational order more appropriate to an interrelated world was being advanced.[22] The United Nations and its specialized agencies were only one manifestation of this higher order. The Council of Europe and the various other European organizations which emerged in the postwar period gave further testimony to the gradual collapse of the old order. Regional alliances on the basis of function or more specifically political were increasingly sought and realized. The older nation-state, built upon its base of sovereign status, has by now lost much of its *mystique* and is perhaps becoming an anachronism. We are witnessing the gradual acceptance of a perhaps more hopeful view which, while it guarantees the sovereign integrity of the state, nevertheless appreciably affects the application and discharge of sovereign functions.[23]

It was in this revised intellectual atmosphere that the African leaders functioned and into this system of world order that the African states were received. In practice, this led the African states to different patterns of behavior as well as different expectations, and the doctrine of the territorially sovereign state was demoted to a position less than ultimate.

The African states that attained their independence in the fifties and sixties not only accepted the limitations on their sovereignty which by then were taken for granted by all other states but, from the very beginning, even while aspiring to independence, harbored an ambition to regroup themselves into larger organizations. Thus no sooner had Guinea and Mali been granted their independence than they sought to merge their separate sovereignties into a higher one. That the experiment failed to strike roots and to sustain the federation in no way detracts from the aspiration itself or from the uniquely benign way in which they viewed their newly sovereign status. By the same token, it is not accidental that a merger between Tanganyika and Zanzibar was effected so soon after their

[22] A good discussion of various transnational views can be found in Ernst B. Haas, *Beyond the Nation State, Functionalism and International Organization* (Stanford: Stanford University Press, 1964).
[23] The desirability of this trend, however, has not gone unchallenged. Soviet writers, among others, allege it to be another way by which the more important Western powers try to impose their will and thereby dominate smaller states. See, for example, V. M. Koretsky, "Fundamental Rights and Duties of the States in International Law," *The Soviet Yearbook of International Law, 1958* (Moscow, 1959), pp. 90-92, and D. B. Levin, "The Contemporary Bourgeois Theories of International Law," *The Soviet Yearbook . . .* , 1959 (Moscow, 1960), pp. 124-25.

independence. We could go on enumerating illustrations drawn from all regions of Africa, but this would serve merely to demonstrate further that sovereignty has a different implication in Africa than it has had elsewhere. Unlike the Asian states or certainly the early European powers, the African states do not look upon sovereignty as a treasure to grasp and guard jealously but rather as a device, a preliminary means toward the achievement of higher objectives.

Other factors, less doctrinal in nature, also prompted the African states to move beyond the simple principle of sovereignty. It is widely recognized, and here we must risk repeating a cliché, that the frontiers of the African states correspond to nothing natural. They were drawn for the convenience of the imperial powers or to compromise claims. Africans as well as non-Africans are keenly aware of this abnormality and certainly view some revision of the frontiers of the present African states as both desirable and possible. The African states appear ready to dismantle them so that they can be redrawn on a more natural and perhaps more realistic basis. If this is an objective, and it has been stated by a number of the states of Africa to be one, then the present frontiers can have none of the sanctity accorded similar frontiers of other states elsewhere. The question of concern is not whether they should be redrawn but how they can be redrawn with a minimum of internal or external difficulties. Certainly the world system is receptive to projected changes, provided they occur peacefully. The objection which would be raised would concern the technique of redrawing, not the underlying necessity. Since this is an accepted objective, obviously, the sovereign status of the state looses much of its *mystique.* It is not an accident that the Charter of the Organization of African Unity, while affirming the sovereign equality of states, equally confirms the desirability, the aspiration, and the legitimacy of regrouping states to create more viable or perhaps more natural entities.[24] Only by such regrouping could the natural links among various African groups, severed by imperial occupation and colonial frontiers, be reestablished and allowed to grow and mature. The gathering of now dispersed groups would go very far towards the reduction of existing tensions and conflicts which pit some African states against each other.

[24] Boutros-Ghali, *op. cit.*

The drive to revise the frontiers, however, is not based only on this "natural" factor. An equally compelling force is the lack of economic viability in many of the present African states. Again this is a specifically African element which in the long run may turn out to be one of the most decisive factors leading to a dismantling of existing frontiers. While some African states may be able to afford their independent existence and exercise a certain measure of authority and influence on an international scale on the basis of their economic strength, the vast majority of the African states certainly cannot exist for long without artificial support from outside competing powers. If the economic ambitions of the African states to attain a decent standard of living for their citizens and to provide the necessary facilities for education and other material ends are ever to be even partially satisfied, drastic measures are necessary to harness existing resources and to find additional ones, even if these can only come from neighboring states. To that extent, pooling of material and human resources among several African states has been an evident solution for some time. For it does not make sense, nationally or internationally, to have states with populations of 200,000 or even a million which totally lack the economic base for statehood and independent existence. What does make sense is their merger with others to create a more viable statehood that would not only benefit the participants but might also tend to reduce areas of competition and instability in the world. To attain this type of merger, however, requires that the doctrine of sovereignty be subordinated. The African states have so far shown a willingness to shed that sovereignty for a continental union, which is undoubtedly the most difficult type to attain. It would seem far more feasible, however, to attain modest regional unions, political or functional, that could deal successfully with the economic limitations of the existing states. It is in the light of the economic difficulties encountered throughout Africa that the drive towards some kind of regional integration assumes its practical possibilities. That the colonial systems of administration and service were in part based upon such conceptions may in the long run add impetus to those measures of integration now being supported on economic or other functional grounds.[25]

The governments' espousal of measures of larger integration and of doctrines which, by their very nature, contravene and transcend

[25] T. M. Frank, *East African Unity Through Law* (New Haven: Yale University Press, 1965).

the limitations of sovereignty, such as the "African Personality" or "Negritude," is perhaps more than matched by a specifically African factor which on the popular level aids immeasurably in the progress of these efforts. It has been suggested that on the whole Africans, whether as a result of their sense of time, their pattern of cultivation and agriculture, or their strong streak of nomadic background, so far have not developed the kinds of feelings and attachments towards the soil which the European and to a lesser degree the Asian peasant developed over the centuries.[26] It is possible that their constant movement across the land led them to develop alternative patterns of loyalty concerned more with groups and persons than with the soil. There is good evidence to support this hypothesis, and if we grant "background" factors their due as determinants of courses of action and patterns of behavior, then it would seem logical for Africans generally to be much less concerned with the frontiers of the state than their counterparts in Europe and Asia. In would therefore be quite feasible for African leaders to work towards the redrawing of their frontiers with a minimum of public opposition, a factor with which all European and Asian states would have to contend if they were to develop similar integrationist policies.

Thus far we have emphasized those factors which militate against adherence to the validity and rigidity of the doctrine of sovereignty which underlies the state system. But there is, of course, the grave danger that with the hardening of the administrative structure of the state the frontiers will be equally hardened by administrative practice; in due course they may acquire the same sacredness and inflexibility which they have elsewhere. Furthermore, states have a curious way of giving rise to institutions and institutional interests which become increasingly entrenched; should this be the case, of course, Africa will fall, much to the chagrin of its leaders, into the same abyss that has been the fate of Europe and Asia. But from the very beginning the leadership of Africa have had not only the vision, commitment, and background to innovate but also a sharp awareness of the inherent limitations and the potential destructiveness of the doctrine of sovereignty and the sovereign state. Whether this will lead them to the successful implementation of broader policies of integration and union only time can tell.

[26] Herbert J. Spiro, *Politics in Africa* (Englewood Cliffs, N.J.: Prentice-Hall, Inc., 1962), pp. 130-31.

VII – *The Authenticity of Programs*

All these combined qualities of African nationalism, especially when contrasted with the Asian example, make it unique and perhaps condition the direction it will take in the future. They have given African nationalism a scope much less provincial and a vision much broader and more human than any prior manifestation of nationalism. The various concrete programs adopted by the African states themselves reflect the basic authenticity of these qualities. The moral and material support given by Africans to each other's causes as well as their support for man's concern with freedom and equality on a world scale also reflect that authenticity.

In creating the Organization of African Unity with its ultimate objective of union, in their membership in the Afro-Asian Solidarity Conferences, and in their activities in the United Nations, African leaders seem to be putting into effect the program to which they theoretically committed themselves in the pre-independence period. In the course of this, they are trying to evolve a functionally effective principle which would draw the world closer together and perhaps translate into reality an ideal in which "the absolute equality of races, physical, political and social is the founding stone of world and human advancement." [27]

[27] The words are those endorsed by the delegates to the Second Pan-African Congress (London, 1921) quoted by Padmore, *op. cit.*, p. 130.

III

The Challenge of Change:
Japan and Africa

Claude E. Welch, Jr.

By any criterion the transformation of Japan in the past hundred years stands out as an impressive achievement. In 1868 the country was predominantly agrarian, with limited literacy and little awareness of the outside world. Japan is now a highly industrialized country—the world's largest producer of television sets, the leading builder of ships, the third greatest producer of steel. Ambassador E. O. Reischauer has underlined these accomplishments and their potential relevance to developing countries. "Japan stands out in the history of modernization in the world as a unique case," he notes, "the one non-Western nation that started to modernize vigorously in the nineteenth century and has been ever since lengthening its lead over the other late starters. . . . Its history of modernization should be of particular relevance to the other non-Western nations now seeking to modernize. . . . Modern Japanese history should be their best textbook for its successes and its failures." [1]

Despite such obvious success, the Japanese accomplishment has

CLAUDE E. WELCH, JR., *graduated* magna cum laude *from Harvard College in 1961 and completed graduate work at Oxford University. His doctoral dissertation was a study of four attempts to achieve suprastate political union in West Africa,* Dream of Unity: Pan-Africanism and Political Unification in West Africa *(1966). He is also the editor of* Political Modernization, *a book of readings in comparative political development.*

[1] Quoted by Douglas H. Mendel, Jr., "Japan as a Model for Developing Nations," paper presented at the annual meeting of the American Political Science Association, Sept. 8, 1965.

received little attention in Africa. Rather than study the reasons for the efficiency of Japanese industry, African leaders penalize this efficiency through import quotas and other restrictions in order to rectify unfavorable balances of payments. Japanese aid, though growing in volume, has made little apparent impression south of the Sahara. The twentieth-century development of China and the Soviet Union, as well as the earlier modernization of Western Europe and North America, have been seriously studied in contemporary Africa. On the other hand, the dynamics of Japanese modernization have remained the preserve largely of Western academics, not of the leaders and practitioners of African development.

In this paper I propose to examine some of the political implications of the Meiji Restoration of 1868, then contrast these findings with contemporary developments in Africa. The common analytical factor linking Japan of the 1860s and Africa of the 1960s will be the desire for modernization. This historical exercise is designed to illustrate both the possible applicability of the Japanese experience to Africa (the potential extent of repetition) and the factors unique to each of the two areas (the realm of innovation).

I – Political Modernization and Development

Analysts of development frequently dichotomize between traditional, agrarian societies and modern, industrial societies. The distinctions extend to all aspects of daily life.[2] In traditional societies, a man's position is largely determined by his birth; social relations are strongly influenced by kinship, caste, clan, or ethnic considerations. In modern societies, more stress is laid upon a man's achievement and his potential than upon his ethnic background; social relations depend to a greater degree upon universalistic norms (applicable to all individuals) than upon ascriptive norms (applicable to a single person on the basis of his family background). Social mobility in modern societies tends to be relatively high, but far more limited in traditional societies. Occupational differentiation, while relatively simple and stable in traditional societies, becomes far more marked in modern societies, with the specialization of

[2] Based on F. X. Sutton, "Social Theory and Comparative Politics," in Harry Eckstein and David E. Apter, eds., *Comparative Politics*, (New York: Free Press of Glencoe, Inc., 1963), p. 71. Also see Fred W. Riggs, "Industria and Agraria," in William J. Siffin, ed., *Toward the Comparative Study of Public Administration* (Bloomington: Indiana University Press, 1959), pp. 23-116, for an elaboration of the dichotomy.

labor and the development of complex, bureaucratized organizations. Modern societies are based upon the prevalence of associations (interest groups, trade unions, and the like) that are functionally specific and not dependent upon ascription; traditional societies lack such associations, since custom and social rank dictate a person's position in most interactions. In the social sphere, accordingly, modernization involves shifts from ascription to achievement, from ethnic group to association, from psychic and physical immobility to empathy[3] and social mobility. Diverse populations are integrated; the "fatherlands" of the various social groups coalesce, through various means, into a "nation."

Political modernization involves a variety of analogous developments. The political structure becomes increasingly differentiated, with functionally specific political roles allocated in terms of achievement rather than ascription. The bureaucracy becomes professionalized, with greater emphasis given to rational, scientific, and secular techniques of decision-making. Central administrative, legal, and political activities are extended to and permeate all parts of the society. Popular interest and involvement in the political system increase—though not necessarily involvement in decision-making. The net result is the establishment of a political system capable both of coping with change and of inducing change,[4] based upon the "systematic, sustained and purposeful application of human energies to the 'rational' control of man's physical and social environment." [5] Political modernization, accordingly, measures the capacity of political institutions in dealing with the demands placed upon them. By using a "developmental approach" to political modernization[6]—in other words, by examining the responsiveness and capability of such institutions over an extended period—the various patterns of modernization will become clearer.

[3] Daniel Lerner, *The Passing of Traditional Society: Modernizing the Middle East,* (New York: Free Press of Glencoe, Inc., 1958), pp. 47-54.

[4] S. N. Eisenstadt, "Initial Institutional Patterns of Political Modernization," *Civilizations,* XII, No. 4, (1962), 462. Cf. the definition of *institutionalization* used by Samuel P. Huntington, "Political Development and Decay," *World Politics,* XVII, No. 3 (1965), 393-405. Both articles are reprinted in my reader, *Political Modernization: Readings in Comparative Political Development* (Belmont, Calif.: Wadsworth Publishing Co., 1967).

[5] Benjamin Schwarz, Hakone conference paper, quoted in Marius B. Jansen, ed., *Changing Japanese Attitudes Toward Modernization* (Princeton: Princeton University Press, 1965), p. 23.

[6] Gabriel A. Almond, "A Developmental Approach to Political Systems," *World Politics,* XVII, No. 2 (1956), 183-214.

It is clearly unjustified to define political modernization as the mere adoption of methods and norms of bureaucratic performance prevalent in highly developed Western countries.[7] *Modernization* and *westernization* are not necessarily synonymous.[8] An equation of modernization with industrialization, even if industrialization is defined in the widest possible terms, tends to mistake a part for the whole.[9]

Equally, certain indices (urbanization, literacy, social mobility, exposure to mass media, and the like) can measure the alterations connected with social mobilization,[10] but cannot indicate by themselves whether political development, as contrasted with social change, is taking place. It is my contention that the comparative study of modernization in Japan and Africa must give fundamental attention to the role of the government, the prime instrument for the "systematic, sustained and purposeful application of human energies . . . ," and to the level of institutionalization of the political system.[11]

The process of modernization in many states is marked by the conscious utilization of governmental powers for the achievement of a wide-ranging social, economic, and political revolution. Modernization in non-Western territories may be a phenomenon primarily of the twentieth century when, in bald terms, governments (1) become endowed with the technological capability to carry out sweeping changes in wide realms of social life and (2) are willing as well as able to attempt fundamental transformations. As Manfred Halpern has argued, "the revolution of modernization involves the transformation of all systems by which man organized his

[7] Joseph La Palombara, *Bureaucracy and Political Development* (Princeton: Princeton University Press, 1963), pp. 34-61.

[8] For a contrary view see Dankwart A. Rustow, "Politics and Westernization in the Near East," in Richard H. Nolte, ed., *The Modern Middle East* (New York: Atherton Press, 1963), pp. 57-93.

[9] I take issue here with Wilbert E. Moore, who, following the convention of dealing with modernization in terms primarily of economic development, equates modernization with industrialization: "the extensive use of inaminate sources of power for economic production, and all that that entails by way of organization, transportation, communication, and so on." Wilbert E. Moore, *Social Change* (Englewood Cliffs, N.J.: Prentice-Hall, Inc., 1964), pp. 91-92.

[10] Karl W. Deutsch, "Social Mobilization and Political Development," *American Political Science Review*, LV, No. 3 (1961), 493-514.

[11] Huntington *op. cit.*, pp. 384ff.

society—the political, social, economic, intellectual, religious and psychological systems." [12]

Historically speaking, the first manifestation of modernization occurred in Western Europe after the Renaissance and the Reformation. The emergence of the scientific outlook—the willingness to revise long-standing concepts, to utilize experiments—brought a fundamental alteration.

> Individualism and reason were the two forces that were now let loose in European society. . . . Men came to believe for the first time that it would be possible to rearrange society on rational principles. . . . All these social, economic, political and cultural revolutions helped to break the "cake of custom" of traditional society, and to create our modern world of incessant change and innovation and of enduring achievements. [13]

The forces unleashed by this transformation soon spread far beyond Western Europe. Other societies were affected, either by the direct imposition of colonial rule or by the indirect threat of such imposition. A major impetus for change in nineteenth-century Japan was fear of intervention by Western states. Unless the Japanese adopted scientific techniques and industrial advances—in short, until they created the hallmarks of modernization in their own country—they were prey for external encroachments and interference.

Ward and Rustow have drawn a convenient distinction concerning types of modernization, particularly relevant to the study of Japan. [14] They distinguish between Western societies in which modernization was internally induced, and certain non-Western societies in which the primary incentive to modernization came from outside through realization of the need to acquire sufficient national stability and strength to protect the societies concerned against political and economic encroachments from more developed Western states. The two states on which these observations are

[12] Manfred Halpern, "Toward Further Modernization of the Study of New Nations," *World Politics,* XVII, No. 1 (Oct. 1964), 173.

[13] I. R. Sinai, *The Challenge of Modernization* (London: Chatto & Windus, Ltd., 1964), pp. 17-19.

[14] Robert E. Ward and Darkwart A. Rustow, eds., *Political Modernization in Japan and Turkey* (Princeton: Princeton University Press, 1964), p. 438.

based, Turkey and Japan, did not experience direct European imperial domination in the nineteenth and twentieth centuries.

It seems advisable to consider a third type of modernization, one that we see now in territories whose boundaries and institutions of government were initially established by a colonial administration —in short, in Africa. Patterns of change in African states may differ markedly from those illustrated in Japan after the Restoration. The "defensive modernization" of Japan succeeded in large measure because of bureaucratic efficiency, social homogeneity, and relative isolation from international pressures. Modernization in heterogeneous African countries may be focused primarily upon the creation of national unity and administrative efficacy, factors that could be taken for granted in nineteenth-century Japan. Fear of Western interference (in the guise of neocolonialism) is not as important a motive for modernization as the desire for nation-building, as the wish to transcend deeply rooted sentiments of kin and group. It is to these contrasts that this chapter is devoted.

II – Modernization in Japan

Numerous studies of Japanese modernization have shown that the process was not initiated solely by governmental fiat after the Restoration of 1868.[15] Rather, the rapid development of Japan in the latter part of the nineteenth century was in large measure the fruit of social and economic changes occurring in the latter part of the Tokugawa period: increasing economic integration among the provinces; growing social mobility, notably within the traditional elite; population expansion; rising literacy rates; and the growth of interest in "Dutch learning," as the Japanese called Western scientific and industrial techniques. Such social changes coincided with growing official awareness of threats posed to Japanese life and customs by the West. Fear of Western interference helped push Meiji leaders toward modernization, toward the conscious adoption of certain Western-developed techniques of social, economic, and political control designed to strengthen the state. "The horrible example of neighboring China haunted all Japanese elites. . . .

---

[15] See, for example, Ronald P. Dore, *Education in Tokugawa Japan* (Berkeley and Los Angeles: University of California Press, 1964), and his "Talent and the Social Order in Tokugawa Japan," *Past and Present*, No. 21, n.d., pp. 60-72; Bernard S. Silberman, *Ministers of Modernization: Elite Mobility in the Meiji Restoration 1868-1873* (Tuscon: University of Arizona Press, 1964); and Robert E. Ward, "Political Modernization and Political Culture in Japan," *World Politics*, XVI, No. 4, 1963, 569-96.

The smoothness of the Meiji restoration was due largely to the shared fears of most Japanese elites in and out of power, and their mutual determination to avoid foreign encroachments." [16] On examination of each of these factors in greater detail, the contrasts and similarities with contemporary African states will become apparent.

Tokugawa Ieyasu (died 1616) sought to establish an effective administrative system that would, after his death, prevent the civil strife that had torn Japan in earlier centuries. He and his followers were eminently successful. The creation of a strong, centralized administration maintained domestic peace and tranquillity, 250 years of calm during which the foundations were laid for the modernization of Japan. National income grew, as did educational facilities; by the seventeenth century "education and learning had become so widespread that there was no dearth of educated men or capable administrators for the Edo [Tokugawa] government." [17] Although government posts were restricted to members of the highest social stratum,[18] merit as a criterion for appointment and promotion was recognized.[19] The social values of Confucianism, deliberately espoused by the Tokugawa, placed the highest premium upon the effective, just, and humane use of power; theoretically, no limitations existed on the scope and powers of the bureaucracy. In retrospect it appears obvious that "the long, gradual process of institutional and attitudinal preparation for modernization . . . was underway at least a century before the Restoration." [20]

National unity developed with the establishment of peace and the imposition of strict social controls. To stave off secessionist tendencies, for example, nobles were required to spend half the year at the Tokugawa court, and to leave hostages. Internal trade flourished through the elimination of many trade restrictions, making Japan an increasingly integrated economic unit. Formerly self-

[16] Mendel, *op. cit.,* p. 9.

[17] Edwin O. Reischauer, *Japan, Past and Present,* 3rd ed., (New York: Alfred A. Knopf, Inc., 1964), p. 85. Also see Ronald P. Dore, "The Legacy of Tokugawa Education," in Jansen, *op. cit.,* 99-131. Dore estimates (p. 100) that 40-50 per cent of Japanese boys and 15 per cent of Japanese girls were receiving some form of formal schooling, which suggests greater literacy than in developing countries at the present time and in most European states at a comparable level of development.

[18] Following the Confucian tradition, social stratification in Tokugawa, Japan was based on a fourfold division: warriors-administrators, (including the *daimyo* and *samurai*), peasants, artisans, merchants.

[19] Thomas C. Smith, " 'Merit' in Tokugawa Bureaucracy," paper prepared for the Conference on Modern Japan, 1963.

[20] Ward, *op. cit.,* p. 577.

sufficient communities were drawn into commercial networks; the cultivation of rice and silkworms increasingly gave merchants a position of economic dominance.

On the other hand, domestic tranquillity undercut the position of the *samurai*, the "feudal retainers" or warrior-administrators. Their economic status declined; they were dependent on fixed stipends measured in *koku* (containers of rice) and fell victims to inflationary pressures. Land and seignorial rights associated with it, which had been widely dispersed among the *samurai*, were consolidated in the hands of a few hundred noble families. As Smith has noted, both the juridical and social ties of the warrior-administrator class with the land were cut.[21] Yet few avenues were open whereby the *samurai* could improve their economic status. To engage in agriculture or commerce would have been demeaning, an implicit rejection of *samurai* status. It was socially more acceptable for *samurai* to seek ways that fell within the traditional norms of the warrior-administrator group, as through, for example, membership in the bureaucracy and pursuit of Western education. Despite the apparent rigidity of the Tokugawa system, accordingly, there was both pressure and opportunity for innovation. Within the bureaucracy could thus be found individuals—mostly lower *samurai*, usually from areas experiencing rapid population growth—with the capacity to undertake a major transformation of the Tokugawa-imposed system.

The impetus for rejecting the outmoded Tokugawa system came with Western pressure for "opening up" Japan. Perry's ultimatum in 1854 and the obvious power of his fleet, combined with subsequent naval bombardments by American, British, French, and Dutch cruisers, shocked many Japanese into realizing the extent of the gap separating their country and its level of technology from the industrialized West. Obviously the Shogunate had outlived its usefulness; this "feudal throw-back," in John Whitney Hall's words, could not cope with the threats posed by the West.[22] In 1867 the Tokugawa Shogun surrendered political control to the fifteen-year-old Emperor. The Emperor exercised little more control than before the "Restoration," but the men ruling in his name were motivated by quite different considerations than the Tokugawa overlords had been.

[21] Thomas C. Smith, "Japan's Aristocratic Revolution," *The Yale Review*, L, No. 3, 1961, 374.
[22] Quoted in Ward, *op. cit.*, p. 574. Cf. the remark of Reischauer: "Despite its continued efficiency, the Edo system had become so hopelessly unsuited to the mentality of the Japanese nation that, once it started to crack, it collapsed suddenly and completely." Reischauer, *op. cit.*, p. 113.

The slogans "Revere the Emperor, Repel the Barbarian" and "Prosperous Nation, Strong Army" exemplify the means and objectives of the Meiji reformers. By stressing national unity and loyalty to imperial symbols, and by working assiduously to achieve the industrial and economic trappings of the contemporary West, the leaders of the Restoration consciously launched Japan into the process of modernization. The "crucial requirement," according to William W. Lockwood, "was the emergence of a new elite with the capacity to face realistically the situation confronting them, to identify their own personal and class interests with the cause of modernization, and to act in the role of leadership before the opportunity was lost." [23]

The Restoration represented a revolutionary change. But the revolution was not carried out, as in Africa almost a century later, by individuals claiming a right to rule based on concepts of popular sovereignty and electoral success. Japan was modernized by an aristocracy willing—like few other governing groups in history— to abolish its own privileges. The sweeping changes instituted by the Meiji reformers represent a unique chapter in history. Thomas C. Smith has called attention to the aristocratic character of the Restoration:

> There was no democratic revolution in Japan because none was necessary: the aristocracy itself was revolutionary. . . . Until 1868, Japan was ruled by a class of knights who alone had the right to hold public office and bear arms and whose cultural superiority the rest of the population acknowledged. A party within this aristocracy of the sword (and swagger) took power in 1868 and embarked on a series of extraordinary reforms. Where there had before been little more than a league of great nobles, they created an immensely powerful central government: they abolished all estate distinctions, doing away with warrior privileges and throwing office open to anyone with the education and ability to hold it; they instituted a system of compulsory military service, although commoners had previously been forbidden on pain of death to possess arms; they established a system of universal public education; and much else. The result was a generation of sweeping and breathless change such as history had rarely seen until this century. I believe, though of course I cannot prove, that these decades brought greater changes to Japan than did the Great Revolution of 1789 to France.[24]

[23] William W. Lockwood, "Japan's Response to the West: The Contrast With China," *World Politics*, IX, No. 1, 37.

[24] Thomas C. Smith, "Japan's Aristocratic Revolution," pp. 370-71.

The Meiji reformers were fortunate in inheriting the Tokugawa bureaucratic system almost intact. Centralized, staffed by experienced and competent men, many of whom were putting to good use their self-acquired knowledge of "Dutch learning," the Japanese bureaucracy proved itself capable of initiating and directing the process of modernization. The group of leaders was relatively small, drawn from the ranks of Tokugawa administrators. The modernization of Japan was accordingly initiated and carried out by the government bureaucracy: neither political parties nor colonial mentors exercised any influence.[25]

The Meiji reformers were similarly fortunate in ruling over a country with a disciplined population and insignificant regional differences.[26] Japanese unity had grown over several centuries; the geopolitical unity of the islands, the single written language, the symbolic importance of the Emperor, and the network of economic exchanges were powerful factors of national integration. Herein lies the key to the relative ease with which modernization occurred in Japan. To quote Reischauer: "By the nineteenth century the Japanese were definitely a nationalistic people, and their possession of a fully developed spirit of nationalism perhaps best explains the success and speed with which they transformed their country into a modern nation-state." [27] Around the imperial symbol the Meiji leaders rallied a substantial degree of support, both by discrediting the Tokugawa "usurpers" and by providing a focus of loyalty for the population. Life in rural areas changed little in the immediate post-Restoration period; by exploiting the countryside, the modernization of the industrial, urban, commercial, and military sectors could be financed.[28] The agricultural population remained placid, loyal to the Emperor, in effect the milch-cow for development in the urban centers.

[25] Although the idea of political parties came to Japan around 1872, it was not until 1889, with the granting of the Meiji constitution and the establishment of the Diet, that parties could operate within an institutional setting. For political development in this period see Robert A. Scalapino, *Democracy and the Party Movement in Prewar Japan: The Failure of the First Attempt* (Berkeley and Los Angeles: University of California Press, 1953), pp. 40-91.

[26] The Satsuma rebellion of 1877 cannot be considered solely as a manifestation of regional differences. Saigo Takamori and his followers in the rebellion were protesting against government measures depriving the *samurai* of their few remaining social privileges.

[27] Reischauer, *op. cit.*, p. 102.

[28] Ward, *op. cit.*, p. 580. In the 1875-79 period, 80 per cent of central government revenues came from land taxes, 60 per cent thereafter Mendel, *op. cit.*, pp. 13-14.

No simple explanation can be advanced for the alacrity with which Japanese leaders plunged into the tasks of modernization. The anachronism of certain Tokugawa attitudes and practices, combined paradoxically with the effectiveness of the administration, a spread of education (both in "Dutch learning" and in the traditional curriculum), a marked increase in social mobility (though largely unnoticed at the time), and growing awareness of Western expansion were pre-Restoration occurrences of immense significance. The Western challenge to Japanese isolation represented, in a sense, the spark that set the timber ablaze. To strengthen the nation and guard against encroachment the Meiji reformers sought to overcome their country's relative backwardness as quickly as possible. That the process was so rapid, so successful that Japan could defeat a major European power less than forty years later, shows the importance of the pre-Restoration foundation for modernization. "The florescence of national leadership during the early Meiji Period, combined with the international circumstances and opportunities of the times, had a great deal to do with the amazing speed at which Japan modernized," Robert Ward has commented, "but in a more fundamental sense Japanese society seems to have been prepared for the experience to a degree still unmatched in some important respects among many contemporary Asian societies." [29] Unmatched, one must add as well, in most contemporary African societies.

III – *Modernization in Africa*

Colonialism initiated the process of modernization in Africa. "Defensive modernization," as shown in Japan following the Restoration, was not feasible south of the Sahara. The government of Japan wished, as did many African groups, to keep the West at arm's length. Three closely related factors, however, brought Africa under European rule. First, the weakening of the balance of power in Europe made Africa the stage on which political rivalries were accommodated. The emergence of Germany as a powerful claimant for territory and the breakdown of the Anglo-French entente following the 1882 occupation of Egypt triggered, as Robinson and Gallagher have noted, "a secondary rivalry for possession of tropical Africa." [30] The European determination to seize huge areas could

[29] Ward, *op. cit.*, pp. 577-78.
[30] Ronald Robinson and John Gallagher, *Africa and the Victorians: The Official Mind of Imperialism* (London: Macmillan & Co., Ltd., 1961), p. 162.

not be stemmed by African resistance. Second, European contact with Africa was far more extensive than with Japan; in many instances, economic relations were gradually transformed into political subordination. The Tokugawa rulers had isolated Japan from the main currents of international trade; Africa, by contrast, was bound to wider markets initially through the slave trade, later through such natural products as ivory, palm products, cocoa, and rubber. Unlike China, with its European-ruled enclaves, and the coast of Africa, with trading and coaling stations, there were no territorial holdings in Japan from which European hegemony might have been extended. But perhaps the most important factor was the tremendous disparity in military power and technology between African and European forces. Given the Western desire to "pacify" Africa—a feeling not expressed for Japan—and the gross technological inequality, the eventual elimination of most open African resistance to Western rule was a foregone conclusion.

The imposition of colonial rule brought social change and differentiation of a substantially new character to Africa. Physical intrusion, economic example, and the communication of skills and ideas, to adopt a classification suggested by an M.I.T. group of consultants, dramatically speeded up the process of modernization. "It was the nature of the colonial experience," these scholars observed, "that at every level of life it brought to the traditional society contact with some degree of modernization." [31] The changes introduced or intensified by foreign rule are familiar to all students of African politics: urbanization, increased mobility, the weakening of traditional values of solidarity, the expansion of education. New patterns of trade and development, a stress upon cash crops, and the imposition of taxes payable in cash rather than in kind resulted as well from colonial administration. For purposes of this analysis, however, the most noteworthy effect of European rule came in the political realm. "Nationalism"—the desire to achieve self-government, in its simplest expression—resulted from the delimitation of new territorial units and the gradual growth of "national" consciousness within these units. This process of territorial nationalism has been cogently described by Apter and Coleman:

[31] *United States Foreign Policy: Economic, Social and Political Change in the Underdeveloped Countries and Its Implication for United States Policy*, Report Submitted to the United States Senate Committee on Foreign Relations by the Massachusetts Institute of Technology, quoted in Roy C. Macridis and Bernard E. Brown, eds., *Comparative Politics: Notes and Readings* (Homewood, Ill.: Dorsey Press, 1964), p. 622.

The net effect of European colonialism in Africa has been to create—albeit unwittingly—embryonic nations coterminous with boundaries of the colonial administrative units. Despite the brevity of European rule, a variety of historic integrative processes have operated within the confines of those boundaries to create, at least among certain strata of the population, a sense of national consciousness. The mere fact of establishing a common administrative and judicial system, common representative institutions, a common communication and transportation grid, a common educational system and acculturative process, and of providing a lingua franca, among many other things, served to differentiate the peoples inhabiting one territory from those in another. Territorial differentiation has been further strengthened by the consequentially greater interaction and communication among the peoples of one territory as against those in other territories. All of these factors have operated to create a "territorial" as distinguished from an "African" personality.[32]

One must quickly add that the forces creating a "territorial" personality have to a certain extent undercut traditional social loyalties based (in most instances) on lineage, ethnic group, or the like. The process, however, is far from complete, and the unsolved question of national identity may be the fundamental problem of modernization in contemporary Africa.

Rather than recount in detail the multifaceted impact of colonialism and the development of anticolonial movements, I prefer to concentrate on the period since independence. All African leaders subscribe to the idea of progress, of modernity, of industrial growth and territorial integration. "A better way of living through nationalism" aptly summarizes their credo.[33] Nationalism is a social value, a feeling of solidarity among diverse groups which, until European conquest, may have had little in common.[34] Yet how

[32] David E. Apter and James S. Coleman, "Pan-Africanism or Nationalism?" in American Society of African Culture, *Pan-Africanism Reconsidered* (Berkeley and Los Angeles: University of California Press, 1962), pp. 92-93. For a detailed analysis of the effects of "territorialism" in four attempts to achieve suprastate political union in West Africa, see my *Dream of Unity: Pan-Africanism and Political Unification in West Africa* (Ithaca: Cornell University Press, 1966).

[33] Here I am combining two of Silvert's four categories: nationalism as ideology, and nationalism as social value. ". . . Political thought concerning what the nation was, is, and ought to be . . . that norm defining the loyalty due to fellow citizens and to the mandates of the state, the tacit consent extended to the activities of the state within the national society, and the internalized 'feeling' of national community." K. H. Silvert, ed., *Expectant Peoples: Nationalism and Development* (New York: Random House, Inc., 1963), p. 18.

[34] Emerson's observations on this point are particularly apt:

strong are these bonds of solidarity? What obstacles do sentiments of ethnic unity place in the path of modernization? Conversely, in what ways might "tribalism" serve, as former Nigerian President Nnamdi Azikiwe emphasized, as a "pragmatic instrument for national unity"? In this section I shall argue (1) that the enhancement of national unity is a significant part, though by no means the totality, of the process of modernization in Africa, and (2) that the interrelationships of nationalism, tribalism, and modernization are exceedingly complex. It is temptingly easy to equate nationalism and modernization, to assume that tribalism inherently undermines the unity purportedly acquired through nationalism. But like many simple statements, the exceptions and qualifications nearly outweigh the proofs.

For most Africans it is fair to assume that traditional social loyalties to kin and ethnic group outweigh nascent feelings of nationalism. The acceptance of the state as the impersonal and ultimate arbiter of human affairs—to utilize Silvert's definition[35]—is far from complete. Admittedly, the assessment of the relative importance of tribal and national loyalties is exceptionally difficult. Few scholars have the training or financial resources, for example, to test these loyalties through survey techniques. Nevertheless, let us proceed on the assumption that the relative speed and ease of modernization depends to a significant extent upon traditional values. Eisenstadt has commented, "All traditional or tribal frameworks are necessarily the most significant determinants of the degree of adjustment or adaptation to modern conditions." [36]

> It might, indeed, be argued with only slight exaggeration that the nations [in Africa] so far exist only in the persons of the nationalists themselves since they are the only people who have moved beyond the tribal horizons and have come to a broader sense of the society in which they live. The mass of the population in whose name they continue to speak continues to be divided into tribes which are bound together by little, if anything, in the way of language, religion, culture, or shared historical experience. The one common aspect of their lives has been the brief subjection to European rule, and this, for the bulk of them, has often meant virtually nothing in the way of a common life.

Rupert Emerson, "Nationalism and Political Development," *Journal of Politics,* XXII, No. 1 1960, 17. See also Professor Emerson's *From Empire to Nation: The Rise to Self-Assertion of Asian and African Peoples* (Cambridge, Mass.: Harvard University Press, 1960), pp. 153-54.

[35] Silvert, *op. cit.,* p. 19.

[36] S. N. Eisenstadt, "Social Change and Modernization in African Societies," in William H. Lewis, ed., *French-Speaking Africa: The Search for Identity* (New York: Walker & Co., 1965), p. 233.

The ethnic heterogeneity of African states is frequently cited as a basic obstacle to modernization. Diatribes against tribalism recur, with almost monotonous regularity, in the writings of many prominent African spokesmen.[37] Their concern is with unity, thereby reflecting their belief that such "primordial sentiments" [38] inevitably detract from the tasks of nation-building. To weld together "a melange of peoples of widely varying primordial attachments into a new and larger 'terminal community' " [39] appears to be the basic task, without the accomplishment of which modernization cannot proceed either rapidly or efficiently. Ethnic sentiments, as Geertz notes, may be quickened, not quieted, by political modernization. His compelling argument runs in these terms:

> The transfer of sovereignty from a colonial regime to an independent one is more than a mere shift of power from foreign hands to native ones; it is a transformation of the whole pattern of political life, a metamorphosis of subjects into citizens. . . . This thrusting of a modern political consciousness upon the mass of a still largely unmodernized population does indeed tend to lead to the stimulation and maintenance of a very intense popular interest in the affairs of government. But . . . much of this interest takes the form of an obsessive concern with the relation of one's tribe, region, sect, or

[37] The resolution on "Tribalism, Religious Separatism, and Traditional Institutions" passed at the 1958 All-African Peoples Conference exemplifies such a view:

> . . . tribalism and religious separatism are evil practices which constitute serious obstacles to
> (i) the realisation of the unity of Africa;
> (ii) the political evolution of Africa;
> (iii) The rapid liberation of Africa. . . .
> And whereas some of these [traditional] institutions actually support colonialism and constitute the organs of corruption, exploitation and repression which strangle the dignity, personality and the will of the African to emancipate himself,
> Be it resolved that those African traditional institutions whether political, social or economic which have clearly shown their reactionary character and their sordid support for colonialism be condemned.

Reprinted in Colin Legum, *Pan-Africanism: A Short Political Guide* (London: Pall Mall Press, 1962), p. 235.
[38] Clifford Geertz, "The Integrative Revolution: Primordial Sentiments and Civil Politics in the New Nations," in Geertz, ed., *Old Societies and New States: The Quest for Modernity in Asia and Africa* (New York: Free Press of Glencoe, Inc., 1963), pp. 105-57.
[39] James S. Coleman and Carl G. Rosberg, Jr., eds., *Political Parties and National Integration in Tropical Africa* (Berkeley and Los Angeles: University of California Press, 1964), p. 688.

whatever to a center of power that, while growing rapidly more active, is not easily either insulated from the web of primordial attachments, as was the remote colonial regime, or assimilated to them as are the workaday authority systems of the "little community." Thus, it is the very process of the formation of a sovereign civil state that, among other things, stimulates sentiments of parochialism, communalism, racialism, and so on, because it introduces into society a valuable new prize over which to fight and a frightening new force with which to contend.[40]

The major point is that the transfer of loyalties from tribe to nation is not a one-step process. "Detribalization" does not automatically entail a sense of deep, abiding awareness of national ties. Rather, there are two steps: the weakening of traditional bonds of social solidarity, and the reintegration of such detribalized individuals into larger social units. Deutsch has called this "social mobilization," "the process in which major clusters of old social, economic and psychological commitments are eroded or broken and people become available for new patterns of socialization and behavior." [41] Unity within a culturally heterogeneous state may be threatened by social mobilization; by contrast, a relatively homogeneous state like Japan will be further consolidated. "Other things assumed equal," Deutsch notes, "the stage of rapid social mobilization may be expected, therefore, to promote the consolidation of states whose peoples already share the same language, culture, and major social institutions; while the same process may tend to strain or destroy the unity of states whose population is already divided into several groups with different languages or cultures or basic ways of life." [42] Little wonder, then, that African political leaders bend their efforts toward eradicating—or at least minimizing—the importance of ethnic sentiments. Far from eliminating these loyalties, modernization may stimulate them. Eisenstadt has written of the "persistence, transformation, and structural recrystallization of various traditional forms and frameworks" [43]—a development to which the burgeoning of nationalist political parties must not blind us.

Colonialism thus accelerated the process of social change manifested (notably after World War II) in the rise of nationalist movements. Modernization helped bring nationalism. At the same time, however, it did not bring a complete disengagement from tradi-

[40] Geertz, op. cit., pp. 119-20.
[41] Karl W. Deutsch, op. cit., p. 494.
[42] Ibid., p. 501.
[43] Eisenstadt, op. cit., p. 230.

tional bonds of social solidarity—in short, from the thrall of "primordial sentiments." Modernization has transformed ethnic loyalties, as well as vitiated them. The effects of the imperfect nature of national unity are described in the following section.

IV – *Traditionalism in Japan and Africa*

The most marked contrast between Japan in 1865 and African states in 1956 can be traced in the degree of their social and cultural heterogeneity. It is a truism that African countries are not yet nations; rather, each resembles collections of "fatherlands," brought together into a single political system through the aegis of European colonialism[44] and the activities of political parties. Japan represents the opposite case. Centuries of isolation from invasion, a racially homogeneous population (99.3 per cent pure in terms of racial composition),[45] a single script and only minor regional dif-

[44] La Patrie, c'est l'héritage que nous ont transmis nos ancêtres: une terre, un sang, une langue, du moins un dialecte, des moeurs, des coutumes, un folklore, un art, en un mot, une culture enracinée dans un terroir et exprimée par une race. . . . En Afrique occidentale, la Patrie, c'est le pays *sérère*, le pays *malinké*, le pays *sonhraï*, le *mossi*, le *baoulé*, la *fon*.

La Nation, si elle rassemble les patries, c'est pour les transcender. Elle n'est pas, comme la Patrie, déterminations naturelles, donc expression du milieu, mais volonté de construction, mieux de reconstruction. . . . Au terme de sa réalisation, la Nation fait, de provinces différentes, un ensemble harmonieux: un seul pays pour un seul peuple, animé d'une même foi et tendu vers un même but. . . .

Si la Nation est volonté consciente de reconstruction, l'Etat en est le moyen majeur. L'Etat est à la Nation ce que l'entrepreneur est à l'architecte.

("The Fatherland is the heritage our ancestors transmitted to us: a land, a blood, a tongue or at least a dialect, habits, customs, tradition, art, in a word, a culture rooted in a soil and expressed by a race. . . . In West Africa, the Fatherland is the *Serer* country, the *Malinké* country, the *Songhai* country, the *Baoulé*, the *Fon*.

The Nation, if it brings together the fatherlands, does so to transcend them. It is not, like the Fatherland, a natural expression and thus an expression of the setting, but the desire for construction, better for reconstruction. With the completion of its realization, the Nation makes a harmonious whole of different provinces: a single country for a single people, animated by the same faith and set toward the same objective.

If the Nation is the conscious desire for reconstruction, the State is the major means of this. The state is to the Nation what the builder is to the architect.—TRANS. BY AUTHOR, C. E. W.)

Léopold Sedar Senghor, *Nation et Voie Africaine du Socialisme* (Paris: Presence Africaine, 1961), pp. 22-24.

[45] Ward, *op. cit.*, p. 582.

ferences in the vernacular, a myth of imperial supremacy traced back to the ninth century A.D., and, under the Tokugawa Shoguns, an efficient central administration had created—as well as reflected —a substantial basis of national unity. The establishment of such uniformities in African states has yet to come. Most African leaders are committed to national unity as "the supreme value and goal." [46] But the goal is at best partially achieved. What the Meiji reformers could take for granted is only nascent or problematic in contemporary Africa.

Central to the modernization of Japan was the Emperor. His purported restoration to power signaled the scraping of obsolete Tokugawa concepts and the adoption of new types of economic, political, and social organization. The imperial symbol, hollow as it may appear in retrospect, helped maintain continuity and preserve loyalty, particularly in rural areas. The cultivation of mass loyalty, obedience, and reverence for the Emperor was doubtless a deliberate attempt by the Meiji leadership to channel popular attitudes in certain directions[47]—an immensely successful step. In African states the relationship between traditional leaders and modernizing government officials is much more ambiguous and fraught with greater tensions than had been the relationship between the Meiji court and the administrators of the Tokyo government. Traditional rulers are often viewed by African officials and party leaders as obstructionist, obscurantist, or divisive, implacably opposed to social and political change. This is a simplification, to be certain, but the fact remains that traditional and modernizing leaders may be competitive in Africa, rather than complementary, as they were in Meiji Japan.

The contrasting roles of traditional rulers in the Japanese and African settings can be attributed to three factors. First, chiefs in African territories are rarely identified with whole states. The Emperor, by contrast, reigned over all Japan, not over a small portion. It would be extremely difficult to find a comparable situation in Africa. All African states contain a variety of ethnic groups; to choose the symbols and leadership of one such group for the whole territory could arouse suspicion of attempted dominance. Ethno-

---

[46] Coleman and Rosberg, *op. cit.*, p. 663. This commitment is paralleled by a strong belief in African unity, although there are as many roads to interstate unity as to intrastate unity.

[47] Ward, *op. cit.*, pp. 579-80.

centrism and national unity are obvious rivals in the heterogeneous societies of modern Africa.

Secondly, colonial administration discredited many African traditional leaders in the eyes of the nascent political elite. In French-ruled territories, where the *chefs de canton* were regarded as cogs in the administrative machinery—as tax collectors, as purveyors of laborers and soldiers, and the like—their bases of societal support were weakened.[48] Comparable events occurred in British Africa. In opposing European rule party leaders opposed its agents, the chiefs. Tarred with the colonialist brush, often more dependent for support on the European administration than on their own peoples, the chiefs were threatened by the development of political protest movements. As a result, in the later period of colonial administration chiefs were instrumental in forming and supporting parties opposed to rapid political advance and to the forces of modernization embodied in mass-based parties.[49]

The development of the French Soudan (now the Republic of Mali) aptly illustrates the political cooperation of administrators with "straw" parties. The leader of the *Parti Progressiste Soudanais* (PSP) Fily-Dabo Sissoko, courted official favor; his party represented established forces within the political system.[50] The *Union Soudanaise* leaders "saw both the administration and the PSP as facets of the same enemy, an enemy that meant 'colonialism,' economic and social domination, and political oppression." [51] Ani-

[48] "Le chef n'est pas considéré comme un potentat mais comme un auxiliaire administratif utile." ("The chief is not considered to be a potentate but a useful administrative auxiliary."—TRANS. BY AUTHOR, C. E. W.) Hubert Deschamps, *L'Eveil politique africain* (Paris: Presses Universitaires de France, 1952), p. 81.

[49] See, for example, Ruth Schachter Morgenthau, *Political Parties in French-Speaking West Africa* (Oxford: The Clarendon Press, 1964), p. 333.

[50] *Ibid.*, p. 284.

[51] Frank Gregory Snyder, *One-Party Government in Mali: Transition Toward Control* (New Haven: Yale University Press, 1965), p. 65. Also note Zolberg's observation on the Ivory Coast:

. . . the activities of the P.D.C.I. cadre and rank-and-file drove many chiefs, who had earlier participated in the [electoral] alliance, into the arms of the French administration to obtain protection. . . . Many individual chiefs became active in parties sponsored by the administration to offset the P.D.C.I.

Aristide R. Zolberg, *One-Party Government in the Ivory Coast* (Princeton: Princeton University Press, 1964), p. 120.

mosities between party officials of the *Union Soudanaise* and many
traditional leaders formerly associated with the PSP have yet to be
fully assuaged; the position of the chiefs in contemporary Mali is
undoubtedly affected by the preindependence alliance of French
administrators with traditional rulers.

The third factor, closely connected with the second, concerns the
amount of power wielded by traditional rulers after independence.
In Meiji Japan, as in Tokugawa Japan, the Emperor reigned
but did not rule. Though influential in symbolic fashion, he could
not and did not exercise direct control over any significant part of
the political system. The court was manipulated by Meiji leaders,
as already noted, to enhance the process of modernization. Tradition was not seen as incompatible with social change. Despite the
immense transformations that have occurred in Africa in recent
years, it would be inaccurate to claim either that traditional rulers
have been divested of power or that they wholeheartedly support
government policies. Chiefs continue to enjoy considerable influence and prestige in most African societies, and therefore they represent a potential threat to political leaders. Their long-standing
social eminence could, under certain conditions, be converted into
strong challenges to party heads. Often a *modus vivendi* is reached
between politicians and chiefs, to be sure, yet the fact remains that
traditional leadership has generally not been identified with modernization in Africa.[52] Traditional leadership in Japan legitimized
and eased the transition from Tokugawa to Meiji systems, but independence in African states, particularly when accompanied by rapid
social change, often lacked the unstinting cooperation of the chiefs.
The Emperor was not politically controversial because the Kyoto
court had been effectively isolated from the exercise of power for
centuries; he could easily be accepted, and utilized, by the reformers.
On the other hand, many African traditional leaders were either
associated with the colonial administration or involved in what
nationalist leaders considered inappropriate political activities.

The comparison should not be pressed too far, however. Although
differences arose between many anticolonial leaders and chiefs before independence, it should not be assumed automatically (1) that
all traditional rulers opposed nationalist movements, (2) that the
growth of political parties entailed a rejection of traditional heri-
tages, or (3) that the chiefs usually did not support party leaders

[52] A striking exception to this generalization, the kingdom of Buganda, is
discussed below.

after independence. Close study of any African anticolonial movement will reveal that many chiefs spread the gospel of anticolonial-
ism. Traditional social eminence did not preclude active participation in or support for political parties seeking rapid independence.
Traditionalistic elements can readily be found in the pomp and
regalia of all African political movements, regardless of their ideologies and outlooks. The Convention Peoples Party (CPP) in
Ghana, before its dissolution after the 1966 military coup, incorporated such elements as linguists, libation-pouring, and invoca-
tions into its public ceremonies. The walking stick of Julius Nyerere
—a symbol of age and leadership in East Africa—gives him an
aura of authority recognized by all citizens of Tanzania.[53] The
point is that to establish anticolonial united fronts it was necessary
to utilize traditional elements readily understood by the masses.
Friedland makes this point forcefully:

> Traditional elements could also be taken over quite consciously by
> the anti-colonialist movements in attempts to broaden the base of
> these movements. These movements had originated with westernized
> Africans and adaptations had to take place as an appeal was made to
> more parochial and tribally-minded Africans in the rural areas. Thus,
> specific elements of traditional society were manipulated to broaden
> the appeal of the anti-colonialist movements.[54]

A significant contrast between Meiji Japan and contemporary
Africa can be traced in the role of political parties and the extent
of political participation. The Restoration and the post-1868 modernization of Japan were led by a small, relatively cohesive group
of men who rose through the administrative hierarchy. The governmental bureaucracy was the instrument by which the goal of a
strong and wealthy nation was pursued. Parties were extremely
weak; not until the granting of the Meiji Constitution in 1890 did
the Diet (parliament) come into existence. Without elections political parties had no firm basis from which to grow.[55] Meiji Japan

---

[53] William H. Friedland, "Some Sources of Traditionalism Among Modern
African Elites," reprinted in William John Hanna, ed., *Independent Black
Africa: The Politics of Freedom* (Chicago: Rand McNally & Co., 1964), p. 364.
 [54] *Ibid.*, p. 367.
 [55] The significance of constitutional and electoral reform in promoting the development of African political parties has frequently been noted. To quote
James S. Coleman:

> The really decisive factor—the precipitant—in the formation of political
> parties has been constitutional reform providing for (1) the devolution by the

was a state firmly controlled by bureaucrats, responsible in their use of power and resources, but responsive to only a limited range of public pressures. The long-standing ethic of the *samurai* warrior-administrators justified their Eastern version of *noblesse oblige*.[56]

Political modernization in Africa has tended to be linked much more closely with parties than with the bureaucracy, although this situation is changing. The "political kingdom" seeks its *raison d'être* in social change, economic development, national unity, all under close direction. These goals have been articulated by party officials, and the parties themselves have been major instruments in striving toward these objectives.[57] I do not wish to press this point too far. The post-independence period has been marked by the increased prominence of formal bureaucratic structures, thereby weakening the governing parties at a crucial moment of transition.[58] Nevertheless, political parties seek to promote, in an active fashion indeed, greater public awareness of social change and to inculcate national unity. Popular apathy is not viewed as advantageous. Rather, stress is placed on participation,[59] on public support for the dominant party, on rejecting cultural pluralism based on tradition. Creation of consensus absorbs the energies of political leaders.[60]

---

imperial government of a sufficiently *meaningful* and *attractive* measure of power to induce or to provoke nationalist leaders to convert their movements into political parties and (2) the introduction or refinement of institutions and procedures, such as an electoral system, which would make it technically possible for parties to seek power constitutionally.

James S. Coleman, "The Emergence of African Political Parties," in C. Grove Haines, ed., *Africa Today* (Baltimore: Johns Hopkins Press, 1955), p. 234.

[56] By the time of the Restoration, "qualities of the ideal bureaucrat had come to be viewed as the very essence of the warrior." Smith, "Japan's Aristocratic Revolution," p. 376.

[57] It is significant, for example, that the "Programme for Work and Happiness" in Ghana was issued by the C.P.P., not by the government.

[58] Coleman and Rosberg, *op. cit.*, p. 674.

[59] See, for example, Zolberg's analysis of the "plebiscitary character" of elections, abstention from which is seen as embodying a negative attitude toward the government. Zolberg, *op. cit.*, pp. 268-72.

[60] The leaders who rode into power acrest the independence movement, upon discovering that achievement of its goal has removed their program and their *raison d'être*, impose an artificial consensus upon the society. The objects of this consensus may include the greatness of the leader, the evils of a neighboring state, the vices of neocolonialism, and the benefits of the modernization plan. Artificial consensus is often imposed after the first signs that the earlier

However, to think of political modernization primarily in terms of social change or political participation misses a point of major import. As Samuel Huntington has convincingly demonstrated, the process of modernization (especially by its rapid alterations in social structure, as through the breakdown of traditional devices of cohesion and control, and by its marked increase in political participation) may lead to "political decay." Huntington prefers to focus attention upon institutions: the adaptability, complexity, autonomy, and coherence of political institutions indicate whether political development is occurring.[61] In Meiji Japan the bureaucracy met these criteria. The adaptability of political institutions, in the face of the unprecedented challenge of modernization as previously defined, was particularly noteworthy. Social mobilization was deliberately slowed, as Ward comments: "One of the real keystones to the successful modernization of Japan was the device of holding constant, i.e. traditional, the circumstances of life in rural and agricultural Japan while at the same time developing the urban, commercial, industrial, and military sectors of the society." [62] But where the traditional way of life is both attacked by political leaders and undermined by the rapid extension of education, as in almost all the states of tropical Africa, political decay is the likely price. "Most modernizing countries are buying rapid social modernization at the price of political degeneration." [63]

Much has been written about charisma facilitating the transfer of loyalties from local group to would-be nation-state. Writing about Ghana a decade ago, David Apter underlined how Nkrumah, by becoming a symbol of a free, prosperous, and united country, enhanced social integration. Charisma, as embodied in the CPP leader, "provided a source of orientational and organizational unity, tending to break down the local separatism and lack of consensus which so often is characteristic of newly emergent states. In the development of a national state, charisma appears to be of immediate value in channeling and vitalizing latent political propensities into conscious or manifested activities . . . , transcending localized

---

natural consensus (based on the desirability of independence) is beginning to crumble.

Herbert J. Spiro, *Africa: The Primacy of Politics* (New York: Random House, Inc., 1966), p. 160.

[61] Huntington, *op. cit.*, pp. 393-417.

[62] Ward, *op. cit.*, p. 580.

[63] Huntington, *op. cit.*, p. 415.

cultural limits to a more generalized African Gold Coast definition." [64] As Weber recognized, however, charisma is inherently
short-lived, "efficacious only in short-lived mass emotions of incal-
culable effects." [65] It becomes "routinized," institutionalized in traditional or bureaucratic forms.[66] Weber's own strictures on the
transient nature of charisma—which some commentators on contemporary Africa seem to have overlooked—should make clear that
national unity requires more than the emergence of a messianic
leader. Charisma may indeed facilitate the establishment of unity
at the level of the state; there is little chance, by contrast, that
"routinization" will actually create the consensus Meiji Japan enjoyed without a charismatic figure. And who would rule out the
possibility of a charismatic leader emerging within a tribal rather
than a national political setting? Furthermore, how possible is
routinization, given the sudden collapse of purportedly charismatic
leadership in Ghana? The utility of charisma in modernization still
remains open to scholarly skepticism.

The contrasting Japanese and African attitudes toward traditional leaders and political participation reflect the fundamental
difference elaborated in these pages: the tenuous character of national integration in African states. The attack on cultural pluralism in African countries (through popular mobilization, redefining
the political role of chiefs, and possibly institutionalizing one-party
dominance) will succeed only in the long term. Primordial ties cannot be easily or rapidly extinguished—and they certainly cannot
be ignored.[67] Tradition is a source of diversity, hence (in the view
of African political leaders) productive of discord and disruptive
of modernization. The regional differences in nineteenth-century
Japan were far less pronounced than the ethnic heterogeneity of
contemporary African states; the Meiji reformers could count upon
a high degree of national integration, a shared awareness of Japan
as a single entity, not a conglomeration of rival groups accidentally
contained within the same frontiers.

Yet the appeal to unity, tradition, and strength expressed during

[64] David E. Apter, *Ghana in Transition* (New York: Atheneum Publishers,
1963), pp. 303, 305.

[65] H. H. Gerth and C. Wright Mills, *From Max Weber* (New York: Galaxy
Books, 1958), p. 262.

[66] *Ibid.*, p. 54. See the criticisms of the application, and misapplication, of
charisma expressed by Carl J. Friedrich, "Political Leadership and the Problem
of the Charismatic Power," *Journal of Politics*, XXIII, No. 1, 1961, 3-24.

[67] Coleman and Rosberg, *op. cit.*, p. 691.

the Restoration period may provide a useful comparison with Africa, not in terms of individual states but in terms of individual societies. In other words, modernization *at the level of the ethnic group* (not the would-be nation) could illustrate patterns similar to those of nineteenth-century Japan. One example is particularly apt: Buganda.[68] The Baganda, as Lloyd Fallers has commented, are ideologically the most committed to modernization of all Uganda peoples.[69] Kiganda culture is an amalgam of traditional and Western elements; as in Meiji Japan, there was selective borrowing, in which an appeal to traditional political loyalty and cultural unity facilitated the incorporation of new elements. The Kabaka, like the Emperor, held a pivotal position in the modernization process. Innovation served immemorability; it strengthened the kingship principle—as long as the principle itself was not challenged.[70] Social change could be incorporated without undermining cultural solidarity. The late Kabaka, writing in 1947, pointed out that there was nothing incompatible between "useful" parts of European culture and traditional Kiganda beliefs:

> I have considered it my duty to warn very strongly all members of this young generation of Baganda that while they are legitimately entitled to strive to acquire education and civilization, they should also take very great care that acquisition of Western education and civilization does not destroy their best native traditions and customs, which in my opinion are quite as good as those found among Western civilized countries but which only require developing and remodeling where necessary.[71]

Modernization in Buganda reinforced the position of the Kabaka by encouraging selective cultural borrowing and incorporation of new techniques. Since the focus of change was the ethnic group and

---

[68] In examining the modernization of Buganda, I have drawn primarily upon the following works: David E. Apter, *The Political Kingdom in Uganda* (Princeton: Princeton University Press, 1961), "Contrasting Factors in the Modernization of Ghana and Uganda," *World Politics*, XIII, No. 1, 1960, 45-68; May Edel, "African Tribalism: Some Reflections on Uganda," (*Political Science Quarterly*, LXXX, No. 3, 1965, 357-72); Lloyd A. Fallers, "Ideology and Culture in Uganda Nationalism," (*American Anthropologist*, LXIII, No. 4, 677-86), and Fallers, ed., *The King's Men* (London: Oxford University Press for East African Institute of Social Research, 1964).

[69] Fallers, "Ideology and Culture . . . ," p. 679.

[70] Apter, "Contrasting Factors . . . ," p. 45; *The Political Kingdom* . . . , p. 21.

[71] Quoted in Fallers, "Ideology and Culture . . . ," p. 683.

traditional authority, Kiganda culture remained introspective, even "intensely chauvinistic." [72] Baganda success in fact even impeded national integration in Uganda as a whole. Other ethnic groups resented the relative dominance of Baganda in positions requiring education and similar skills. The political system of Uganda eventually simply could not reconcile Baganda isolation and separatism with the imperatives of domestic unity. Tensions flared up early in 1966. The position of Prime Minister Obote (a non-Muganda) grew increasingly insecure. Faced with apparently growing threats from the army and members of his own Uganda People's Congress, as well as from the Baganda, Obote took preemptive action late in February. He suspended the Constitution and imprisoned five ministers, on the grounds that a substantial threat to the country's security existed. Baganda politicians reacted swiftly. President Edward Mutesa—the Kabaka—objected to the ministers' suspension and the Prime Minister's seizure of all power. The Lukiko (the traditional Buganda parliament) passed two resolutions condemning Obote's actions. Obote thus came into direct conflict with Buganda, breaking the fragile compromise under which the Uganda government had operated since independence.[73] In late May riots broke out in Kampala, the capital of Uganda and chief city of the Baganda. Violent overthrow of the government was threatened. Obote brought in the army, which sacked the Kabaka's palace, leaving hundreds dead, while the Kabaka fled in disguise. In the interest of a unified Uganda, Obote's supporters claimed, the purported attempt at separatism had to be crushed. Thus national unity and ethnic particularism did not mix in Uganda, save under the unusual circumstances of a political compromise effected to hasten independence.

The violent halt to Buganda separatism, even if temporary, has clear implications for other African countries: modernization may actually exacerbate ethnic differences and antagonisms, not simply smooth them over. Cultures differ in their receptivity to change, and since modernization is preeminently a condition of transformation, some cultures may steal the march on others. "Modernizing ethnocentrism," as Clifford Geertz comments, will simplify and con-

---

[72] *Ibid.*, p. 685.

[73] Under the terms of the compromise Obote was both chief executive and leader of the governing Uganda People's Congress. The Kabaka retained his traditional post and served as well as President of the country.

centrate group antagonisms, not eliminate them.[74] Where national unity is precarious, social change, by maintaining and expanding group consciousness, may undermine whatever degree of integration had previously been attained. Political decay may thus result from the process of modernization.

V – Conclusion

To recapitulate, it seems apparent that the political development of Japan depended upon several factors absent from or weak in contemporary Africa. The lack of national integration in African states, contrasted with the homogeneity of nineteenth-century Japan, is the fundamental contrast. No continental African country today can match the social and geopolitical unity of Japan in the Meiji period. Colonial administration brought together numerous peoples in the same territory, but did not create a "nation" within the boundaries of the state. This task has been left to the present generation of political leaders. The Japanese experience seems more relevant to the modernization of individual societies or groups, particularly societies in which tradition can legitimize cultural borrowing, than to the modernization of polyethnic states. Modernization will affect different ethnic groups in different fashions. The result may be a perpetuation, or a reemergence in new guise, of the communal conflicts African leaders wish to eliminate in the interest of national integration. So long as the primary focus of social loyalty is the ethnic group rather than the state, the example of nineteenth-century Japan will have far greater applicability at the ethnic rather than the national level.

The effective, statewide bureaucracy developed by the Tokugawa had the capability of applying governmental powers to aid in the rapid industrialization and more gradual social transformation of Japan. It is open to serious doubt that the administrations of contemporary African states can cope as efficiently with the tasks resulting from policies promoting rapid social change. Increasing political awareness; widespread social mobilization, resulting in new demands; political institutions not characterized by high degrees of adaptability, complexity, autonomy, and coherence; the difficulties in transforming charisma into routine procedures; the potentially

[74] Geertz, *op. cit.*, p. 154.

divisive character of traditional symbols; a relatively low level of consensus in the political community: such are the problems confronting African leaders. These problems may be far less tractable than those confronting the Meiji reformers a century ago.

To close on an untempered note of pessimism about prospects for modernization and political development in Africa would be unwarranted, however. Historical analogy, if pressed too far, obscures rather than clarifies, leaves aside relevant factors in the interest of comparison. African leaders have made abundantly clear their desire for modernization and their willingness to attain this goal in whatever fashion seems most appropriate. With ingenuity and innovation, not by simple repetition, they can solve these problems. The Meiji reformers were quick to seize upon opportunity and to utilize all possible resources, traditional as well as modern. Perhaps a repetition of this clever adaptability would be the most suitable form of innovation.

IV

Borrowed Theory and Original Practice in African Politics

Ali A. Mazrui

Three elements constitute a style of politics: political behavior, political ideas, and the vocabulary of political discourse. If one assessed the Western impact on the development of modern politics in Africa, one would probably find that the West's clearest impact was on the language used in political evaluations. The verbal equipment which the West has bequeathed to Africa ranges from comprehensive concepts like *socialism* and *economic development* to more limited terms of description like *President* and *the vote*. Attempts to coin indigenous words into which such English (or French) terms might be translated only make the Western linguistic impact more pervasive.

The second element constituting a style of politics is the category of ideas. What is meant by *ideas* here is not merely the words which African ideologues might use but the actual meaning they attach to them. It is a cliché that the idea of *democracy*, for example, might vary from country to country, though the word used is the same. If we then accept this distinction between words and ideas, we can proceed to assert that the West's impact on African political ideas is not quite as great as its impact on Africa's political vocabulary. On the contrary, the similarity of vocabulary between Africa and her former rulers disguises important differences in modes of

ALI A. MAZRUI, *the only African contributor to this collection, received his education in Africa, England, and the United States. His article "On the Concept of 'We Are All Africans',"* published in 1963 in the American Political Science Review, *identified him as a perceptive and original student of African political thought.*

thought. Africa is more original in its ideas than the words she uses may tend to suggest.

This is not to deny that colonialism helped to transform Africa's intellectual universe. In fact, the most significant thing about the colonial experience for Africa is that it was at once a political bondage and a mental liberation. We might even say that the colonial fact was the most important liberating factor that the African mind has experienced in historical times.

Yet even if we do concede that colonialism gave Africa new ideas, we ought to distinguish between two senses of *giving ideas*. One is when the same idea passes from a European to an African. The other is when a European idea, or the European impact as a whole, makes an African think of something else altogether—but something which the African would not have thought of but for the European stimulation. In the former case, the idea itself is not new, it is only new to Africa. But in the latter case, the European stimulus becomes the intellectual manure for a flowering of the African mind. What is then produced is, hopefully, an idea which is not only new to Africa but is new in the world.

Much of African writing so far has been less concerned with trying to produce new ideas than with trying to demonstrate how some of the "imported" ideas are actually very old in Africa's own experience. As Julius Nyerere once put it with regard to two comprehensive "Western" concepts,

> We, in Africa, have no more need of being converted to socialism than we have of being "taught" democracy. Both are rooted in our past—in the traditional society which produced us.[1]

This kind of statement is concerned less with asserting Africa's own originality than with denying Europe's. For the nationalist in such circumstances it is better to have a commonplace idea which owes nothing to foreign influence than to invent a new idea under alien stimulation.

But is not the kind of claim which extracts socialism from tribal values itself a form of originality? For an answer let us quote Karl Marx when he retorted to claims made by Russians in his own time:

> A ridiculous prejudice has recently obtained currency that common property in its primitive form is specifically a Slavonic, or even ex-

[1] "Ujamaa: The Basis of African Socialism," in William H. Friedland and Carl G. Rosberg, *African Socialism*, Appendix II (Stanford: Stanford University Press, 1964).

clusively Russian form. It is the primitive form that we can show to have existed among Romans, Teutons, and Celts, and even to this day we find numerous examples, ruins though they be, in India.[2]

What all this means is that the very assertion that socialism is implicit in the collective solidarity of African tribal life itself has analogues in the ideological history of other parts of the world. In a sense, pre-Communist Russia was the first "developing area" to feel a sense of inadequacy in the face of Western achievements. Nineteenth-century Russians were also among the first to talk in terms of moving from primitive collectivism to industrial socialism without passing through the social agonies of the intermediate stages.

But if such important African claims lack originality, where then do we find that elusive quality in African political thought? Where do we find the best African ideas if not in the tracts and speeches in which Africans express them?

The most promising method of ascertaining the operative ideas of African politics is not by studying what Africans say. It is not by studying what Africans do either. It is by trying to determine the precise relationship between what they say and what they are doing. There is a shadowy gap between political language and political behavior which can sometimes be more expressive of political beliefs than either words or deeds on their own. Only by taking a good look at that gap can we comprehend the real nature of the intellectual stimulation which the colonial experience afforded to Africa.

What I propose to examine in this paper are two sets of ideas and their impact on Africa: first, Western liberalism and its transformation, and then the impact of socialistic ideas and the changes they have undergone in African politics. But the interrelationship between these two sets of ideas will also constitute an integral part of my analysis.

I – Liberalism From Britain

In 1954 James S. Coleman asserted that nationalist movements in Africa were "activated by the Western ideas of democracy . . . and self-determination." [3] Whether by accident or design, Coleman was

---

[2] *Kritik* (1859), footnote 1.

[3] "Nationalism in Tropical Africa," *American Political Science Review*, XLVIII, No. 2 (June 1954), 407.

right in putting *democracy* first on his list of influential ideas, and *self-determination* only later. The sense of *democracy* which was influential in British Africa was, as might be expected, the Anglo-Saxon version of the liberal ethic. Leading British philosophers have seldom concerned themselves in depth with issues like the definition of *nation,* or the reality of a *collective soul,* or the concept of *fatherland.* In some ways it is ironic that this should be so. Carlton J. H. Hayes has argued in the following terms:

> By the seventeenth and early eighteenth centuries, national patriotism was developed more generally and more acutely in England than in any other country—more so than in France or Spain or Sweden, and much more so than in Italy or Germany or eastern Europe. Indeed, we may affirm that modern nationalism, as we know it today, has its original seat in England.[4]

Hans Kohn used similar terms in his book on the origins of nationalism.[5]

And yet neither Kohn nor Hayes sufficiently differentiated between national consciousness and nationalism itself. We may define *national consciousness* here as a sense of shared national identity. We may define *nationalism* as a more defensive or more assertive degree of that consciousness. In the course of time England became less nationalistic precisely because it had a more highly developed national consciousness.[6] England did indeed continue to have moments of militant nationalism, but on the whole she came to take her nationhood so much for granted that her philosophers spent relatively little time on it. Instead of meditating about nationhood, the most towering political thinkers in Britain concerned themselves with problems of devising suitable institutions to realize certain individualistic or subgroup values at home.[7]

[4] *Nationalism: A Religion* (New York: The Macmillan Company, 1960), pp. 38-39.

[5] *Idea of Nationalism: A Study of Its Origins and Background* (New York: The Macmillan Company, 1943), pp. 155-83. See also Ali A. Mazrui, *Towards a Pax-Africana: A Study of Ideology and Ambition* (London: Weidenfeld and Nicolson, 1967).

[6] See also my paper "Pluralism and National Integration," *Proceedings of the Colloquium on Pluralism,* University of California, Los Angeles, 1966.

[7] In his book *Prophets and Peoples, Studies in Nineteenth Century Nationalism* (New York: The Macmillan Company, 1947), Hans Kohn selects John Stuart Mill as the "prophet" of British nationalism. Yet Mill was hardly a striking example of a "people's prophet." Of all British thinkers, Burke perhaps comes nearest to eulogizing the virtues of long-established nationhood. But even Burke is a defender more of tradition than of the fatherland, of custom rather than nationality.

Of the Western philosophy available in the original to English-speaking Africans, Anglo-Saxon liberalism constituted the bulk. The result was that the rhetoric of African nationalism in British Africa was not, in fact, filled with repetitions of the term *self-determination*, as might have been expected. More common in the language of nationalism such terms as *individual freedom, democracy*, and *one man, one vote*. That is why Coleman was right in putting democracy before self-determination in order of influence on African political thought. The Anglo-Saxon version of democracy is basically oriented towards individual freedom. The principle of self-determination, on the other hand, is usually oriented towards the freedom of a group. The paradox of the African experience is that nationalism in the continent derived its original intellectual stimulation from an ethic of individualism.

A related reason why African nationalism was generally expressed in terms of institutional liberalism rather than those of nationality arose out of the British conception of eligibility for independent existence. The principle of national self-determination implies that whoever is "nationally distinct" and wants a separate existence is entitled to it. But the reasoning of British colonial policy was to the effect that independence was not for those who were merely nationally distinct. It was more for those who were capable of maintaining liberal democratic institutions and of safeguarding individual freedom.

In 1962 Nigeria's Nnamdi Azikiwe reminded his countrymen of this British view:

> Thanks to the growth of political consciousness in this country our people are becoming acquainted with the practice of parliamentary democracy. This has been used as a criterion to determine the political maturity of any people under the rule of others and we can be no exception. As a matter of fact, it is a declared policy of Britain that no colony can be considered ready for self-government until it has made parliamentary democracy a political reality.[8]

Azikiwe at that time did not object to this criterion of eligibility for independence. He merely urged his countrymen to put a "full-fledged two-party system in operation."[9] The Anglo-Saxon basis of evaluating political maturity affected Zik's own line of reasoning.

And as late as 1959 this sort of approach to problems of decoloni-

---

[8] *Zik: A Selection From the Speeches of Nnamdi Azikiwe* (Cambridge: Cambridge University Press, 1961), p. 85.
[9] *Ibid.*

zation continued to be discernible in the idiom of British colonial policy. In April 1959 Alan Lennox Boyd, speaking for the Government in the House of Commons, defined British intentions in a colony in the following terms:

> The responsibility of Her Majesty's Government is to all the inhabitants of Kenya. . . . It would be a betrayal of that responsibility if we were to abandon our ultimate authority prematurely. . . . First, there must be in the territory as a whole a sufficient understanding of parliamentary institutions, and sufficient sense of responsibility in public affairs to hold out a reasonable prospect that parliamentary institutions, representative of the people, will produce responsible government. . . . Self-government, I think we would all agree, is but a mockery if it is purchased at the expense of personal freedom.[10]

In the context of such values, capacity for self-government was, in effect, capacity for Anglo-Saxon liberalism. The right to self-government rested on the liberal capacity, and not on national distinctiveness as such.

A third reason why the term *self-determination* was not more in evidence in the earlier days of African nationalism concerns the relative lack of national identity in the individual African territories. The principle of self-determination had too often referred to an old-established nation currently under foreign rule. But Thomas Hodgkin has reminded us that

> There is no African Mazzini; no Gandhi or Sun Yat-Sen. This is not surprising. African nationalism differs from the nationalisms of India and China in that Africa exists as an idea only, projected into the future, not as an historic fact. There has been no single comprehensive civilization, no common background of written culture, to which nationalists could refer.[11]

Demands for self-determination in Europe and to a lesser extent in Asia had often rested on cultural distinctiveness. It is precisely because of this that when the same principle of self-determination was first used to refer to Africa, it was more to the Ashanti than to the Gold Coast that it appeared to be theoretically applicable.

[10] Great Britain, *Parliamentary Debates* (Commons), Vol. DCIV (April 22, 1959), cols. 563-64.
[11] *Nationalism in Colonial Africa* (London: Frederick Muller, 1956; New York: New York University Press, 1957), p. 179.

Since the ethic of self-determination thus seems to connote the freedom of cohesive subgroups, leaders like Tom Mboya have preferred to emphasize instead the rights of individuals regardless of the ethnic group to which they belong. That is why he opposed the idea of regional autonomy as a safeguard of the collective interests of small tribes in Kenya. And that is why he also opposed special safeguards for racial minorities in the country. As he put it once in discussing this latter type of safeguard: "If there are going to be guarantees, they should not be just for Asians and Europeans, but for all of us as citizens of this country." [12] In the same speech Mboya referred to the demand for regional autonomy by Kenya's smaller tribes. He condemned it as a demand for "the fragmentation of Kenya."

As for Mboya's conception of the African struggle as a whole, he described it elsewhere in the neoliberal idiom of being "a struggle . . . based on moral issues and in defence of basic human rights and fundamental freedoms." He urged Africa to assert even after independence a "noble emphasis of dedication to freedom for the individual." [13]

In the colonial struggle, the call for individual freedom still made nationalistic sense in a situation in which the majority of individuals were Africans. And because independence had thus been demanded by appealing to liberal individualism rather than to collective national self-determination, there was no inconsistency after independence in denying self-determination to groups like the Somalis of Kenya or to other such groups. All that the Somalis could demand were their rights as individual citizens of Kenya, not the right of secession or independent existence as a collectivity.

The assumptions of the British liberal ethic thus spared Africa at least one area of ideological dilemma. In short, what Africa voiced was not the demand that every culturally distinct group should determine its own future but simply that there should be "majority rule" in each territorial unit. Independence for a country as a whole could thus be secured without any implicit commitment to give every culturally distinctive group internally an additional right to determine its own independent future.

[12] Speech at a meeting of the United Kenya Club. See *Mombasa Times,* January 11, 1962.

[13] See Mboya, "Vision of Africa," in *Africa Speaks,* James Duffy and Robert A. Manners, eds. (Princeton: D. Van Nostrand Co., Inc., 1961), pp. 24-25.

II – Liberalism From America

But it was not merely from Britain that English-speaking Africa inherited the liberal ethic. It was also from the United States. By no means uniquely, Americans tend to exaggerate the favorable side of their impact on the minds of others abroad. As the United States has grown into a world power, so has this piece of her national vanity—perhaps always ahead of America's real stand in the world. "Everyman," wrote Thomas Jefferson "has two countries —his own and France." "Everyman has two countries," echoed Max Lerner two centuries later, "his own and America." [14]

A less sweeping if still rhetorical claim was the one once made by Chester Bowles in an article in the *New York Times Magazine*. It is a claim that other Americans have made—that the American Revolution was "a revolution intended for all mankind." [15]

One need not accept this assertion in entirety. But in a mood of romantic hyperbole, one could indeed argue that while the French Revolution was the great explosion of democratic ideas, and the Russian Revolution was the great assertion of Marxist ideas, the American Revolution came near to being the great invention of anticolonial ideas and the kind of nationalism which springs therefrom. At any rate, this was the view of Julius Nyerere when he described the occasion of the American Declaration of Independence as "the first time in history that the principles of a struggle for freedom from foreign domination had been clearly defined." [16]

Claims about something being done "for the first time" often contain an element of an exaggeration. Moreover, we can dispute Nyerere's assumption that the American struggle in the eighteenth century was really against foreign domination. The British in the eighteenth century were no more foreigners in American eyes than Harold Wilson was a foreigner to Ian Smith when the latter declared Rhodesia's independence in November 1965. The American War of Independence was indeed a war against colonial rule. What

[14] *America as a Civilization: Life and Thought in the United States Today* (New York: Simon & Schuster, Inc., 1957).

[15] See Chester Bowles, "A Revolution Intended for All Mankind," *New York Times Magazine*, Dec. 10, 1961. For a discussion of the risks of the analogy between Afro-Asian national movements and the American War of Independence, see Herbert J. Spiro, *Politics in Africa: Prospects South of the Sahara* (Englewood Cliffs, N.J.: Prentice Hall, Inc., 1962), pp. 33-35.

[16] Nyerere, "Africa's Place in the World," *Symposium on Africa* (Wellesley, Mass.: Wellesley College, 1960), p. 150.

Africans, Asians, and sometimes contemporary Americans are apt
to forget is that colonial rule need not be foreign rule. The American War of Independence was much more like a civil war than a
war against foreign domination. The rebels were objecting to being
treated like second-class Englishmen. They were demanding the
rights of first-class Englishmen—"No Taxation Without Representation." When they failed to get those rights, they decided that, to
use the words of Thomas Paine, " 'tis time to part!" [17]

When all allowances have been made, however, it still remains
true that the American Revolution has been of some relevance for
the growth of nationalism in Africa. Yet how could an event way
back in the eighteenth century have had any influence on African
militants in the twentieth?

The role of American education for Africans is one important
link. As a Nigerian student dramatically put it two decades ago,
"The first skirmishes in the struggle for political freedom of the
21 million people of Nigeria are being fought in the colleges of
the U.S." [18] This too is a romantic exaggeration. But it is at any
rate substantially true that Africans who were educated in the
United States have tended to be more singleminded in their nationalism than Africans educated in, say, Great Britain. It was
perhaps not accidental that the leadership in Ghana passed from
British-educated personalities to the primarily American-educated
Nkrumah. Nor was it entirely a coincidence that the founding
father of modern Nigerian nationalism was Nnamdi Azikiwe, also
a product of American education.

But what has made American-educated Africans more militant
in their nationalism than British-educated ones? The factor which
is directly linked to the American Revolution is, of course, the
tradition of anti-imperialism which many Americans continue to
subscribe to even if their governments do not always do so. There
is also the derivative factor that America is a more ideological and
more rhetorical country in its politics than Britain usually is. *The
Observer* of London might have been overstating the case when it
described Communist China and the United States as "the two

[17] This point is also discussed in my book *The Anglo-African Commonwealth:
Political Friction and Cultural Fusion* (Oxford: Pergamon Press, 1967).

[18] Prince Okechukwu Ikejiani, "Nigeria's Made-in-America Revolution," *Magazine Digest*, January 1946, p. 57, cited by James S. Coleman, *Nigeria: Background to Nationalism* (Berkeley and Los Angeles: University of California
Press, 1960), p. 244.

most ideologically inspired States of the modern world." [19] But it is certainly true that political beliefs tend to be articulated with greater passion and more hyperbole by Americans than by the British. And exposure to such a climate could make an African educated in the United States more ideological and more rhetorical in his own anti-imperialism than his fellow African educated in the British Isles.

A third factor making education in the United States conducive to African militancy is the race issue. In his book on Nigeria, James Coleman put the question in the following terms:

> The special situation of the American Negro, into whose company an African student is inevitably thrown, was . . . an important conditioning factor. African students in America were perforce made acutely aware of color discrimination, in itself provocative of racial consciousness.[20]

Coleman went on to point out that West Africans did not meet in their own countries the highly institutionalized and omnipresent discrimination characteristic of Southern states, and to a degree also of Northern states, in America. Racial discrimination in Nigeria (formally outlawed in 1948) was irritating mainly as a symbol of European imperialism, but "it did not engulf the individual and plague him at every turn." Thus many Nigerians encountered racial discrimination on a large scale for the first time when they arrived in the United States.[21]

Coleman was on less solid ground when he suggested that the same sort of racialistic cultural shock, though less pronounced, hit an African student studying in England. On the contrary, a reverse type of shock was more usual. What impressed African students in England in those early days was the apparent racial broadmindedness of the British people in England as compared with the type they encountered at home. Many a student came to draw a sharp distinction between these two types of Britons in his experience.

And so, while African students studying in the United States found themselves in a more racialistic society than they had in their colonial homes, African students studying in England found themselves in one less racialistic. This is probably one more reason why

[19] Editorial, *The Observer* (London), May 9, 1965.
[20] *Nigeria: Background to Nationalism*, p. 245.
[21] *Ibid.*

the American-educated African has been the more single-minded in his nationalism.

African attitudes towards the United States are sometimes colored by a feeling of having been betrayed. What then did the Declaration of Independence really mean by "all men are created equal"? Did the Founding Fathers use the argument merely as a debating flourish to justify their unilateral assumption of sovereignty? Was the word *all* in the claim *all men* no more than rhetoric?

It was in the age of Abraham Lincoln that such questions assumed critical importance in the United States. In October 1858—one hundred years before the First Conference of Independent African States and the All African People's Conference held in Accra in 1958—Judge Douglas was arguing to the American electorate that the Declaration of Independence did not include Negroes when it declared all men to have been created equal. This was Judge Douglas' last joint debate with Lincoln. He accused Lincoln of construing the Declaration to include Negroes. The Judge repudiated any such suggestion as "a slander on the immortal framers of our Constitution."

It was this "slanderous" misinterpretation of the intentions of the Founding Fathers which was later to inspire Africans and Afro-Americans. The roots of pan-Africanism do, to a certain extent, lie in the New World. West Indians like Marcus Garvey and American Negroes like W. E. B. DuBois will remain among the founding fathers of pan-African movements. But in those early days Africans, as well as Afro-Americans, were less stimulated by America's assertion of independence from British rule than by America's egalitarian arguments in support of that independence. In other words, African nationalism in its early days drew its inspiration from the unfulfilled part of the American revolutionary aspirations. Even as late as the Fourth Pan-African Congress in 1923 the central aspiration of pan-Africanism was less that black men be given their independence, as the American revolutionaries had got theirs, than that "black folk be treated as men," as the American revolutionaries had implied in their words.

Curiously enough, the Fourth Pan-African Congress was held in both London and Lisbon. London as an imperial capital was later to concede to Africans the right of independence. Lisbon, another imperial capital, was to offer to Africans—too late—active racial equality and assimilation, which was all they had asked for in those early days. If the American Revolution had proclaimed "equality" in pursuit of independence, the African nationalists were now seeking full independence in pursuit of racial equality.[22]

Partly arising out of this African desire for national independence, the bonds between the Negroes of the Old World and the Negroes of the New became weaker. After all, it is not colonialism that the American Negro has been up against; it is a different form of racial handicap. And this difference became important enough to entail different strategies for African nationalism and for the civil rights movement in the United States. It is true that the bonds of shared blackness have far from disappeared even now. Black Rhodesians are among the last Africans to wage a struggle for self-rule. But in spite of their own preoccupations, the one-hundredth anniversary of the Abolition of Slavery in America did not go unnoticed. In September 1962 *Zimbabwe News*, the international organ of a banned African nationalist party of Southern Rhodesia, carried an article entitled quite simply "Abraham Lincoln." The general thesis of the article was that the plight of the American Negro had not improved much since slavery was abolished. This was an exaggeration. But it was an exaggeration arising out of a sense of fellowship between black Rhodesians and black Americans. When all this has been said, however, it remains true that African nationalism is now more preoccupied with peculiarly African matters than with problems of the Negro race as a whole.

This situation has been aggravated by the fall of Nkrumah from power. Kwame Nkrumah might not have been a great Ghanaian, but he was, in a sense, a great Afro-American. No African leader was more conscious of his ties with the black people of America than Nkrumah. As we know, Nkrumah himself was educated in the United States. His activities among American Negroes ranged from dating Negro girls to preaching in Negro churches. The book that had the biggest impact on him in his formative years was, he tells us, the testament of Marcus Garvey, the Jamaican who captured the nationalistic imagination of black people in the United States.

At a state dinner to mark Ghana's independence many years

[22] See also Ali A. Mazrui, "On the Concept of 'We are all Africans'," *American Political Science Review*, LVII, No. 1 (March 1963). For useful accounts of the earlier Pan-African conferences see Colin Legum, *Pan-Africanism* (London: Pall Mall Press, and New York: Frederick A. Praeger, Inc., 1962), and George Padmore, ed., *History of the Pan-African Congress* (London: Hammersmith Bookshop, 1947, 1963).

later, Nkrumah had occasion to recall Garvey. But just before he mentioned Garvey's name to illustrate a point, he used the dramatic device of asking the band to play Ghana's national anthem. Then he made his point, saying:

> Here I wish I could quote Marcus Garvey. Once upon a time, he said, he looked through the whole world to see if he could find a government of black people. He looked around, he did not find one, and he said he was going to create one. Marcus Garvey did not succeed. But here today the work of Rousseau, the work of Marcus Garvey, the work of Aggrey, the work of Caseley Hayford, the work of these illustrious men who have gone before us, has come to reality at this present moment.[23]

Earlier in the same speech Nkrumah reaffirmed the bonds of pan-Negroism in the following terms:

> There exists a firm bond of sympathy between us and the Negro peoples of the Americas. The ancestors of so many of them come from this country. Even today in the West Indies, it is possible to hear words and phrases which come from various languages of the Gold Coast.[24]

In the history of political pan-Africanism perhaps the most important Negroes of the Americas alive in 1957 were George Padmore from the West Indies and W. E. B. DuBois from the United States. To these historic figures Ghana opened her doors on attainment of independence. They died citizens of Ghana. The whole phenomenon was a "Back to Africa" event of unique symbolism.

A year after Ghana's independence Nkrumah visited the United States at the invitation of President Eisenhower. Being his first visit there as Prime Minister of the newly independent Ghana, Nkrumah looked upon the occasion as, in a sense, "the fulfilment of the hopes and dreams of my student days at Lincoln University." Among the places he visited during his stay in the United States was Harlem in New York City. Nkrumah has recorded that "the spectacular and spontaneous welcome given to me by the people of Harlem remains one of the happiest memories of the whole tour."

In the spring of 1961 Nkrumah once again visited Harlem, this time as President of the Republic of Ghana, and addressed a Negro rally there. He reminded his audience that Harlem had once been

[23] Nkrumah, *I Speak of Freedom* (New York: Frederick A. Praeger, Inc., 1961), p. 107. See also Ali A. Mazrui, *Towards a Pax-Africana, op. cit.,* pp. 60-61.

[24] Nkrumah, *ibid.,* p. 91.

a home for him. As a visiting Head of State, Nkrumah was careful about what he said on civil rights in his host country. In fact, he hardly mentioned the specific Negro problem of the United States. To some extent his audience was disappointed. Yet his very presence in Harlem as President of an African country was a moment of excitement to the audience and to Nkrumah.[25]

Nkrumah has now fallen.

In their crisis of identity the Negroes of the United States sometimes feel a need for a sense of pride in their origins. They want to be proud of Africa. But which Africa? Is it just the concept of Africa? How can one be proud of a mere abstraction?

For intellectuals perhaps one can only be proud of an abstraction—a romantic abstraction. Once one comes into contact with reality, the pride receives a shock.

This might be the attitude of intellectuals. But the ordinary Negro people in the Americas often need a little more substance in their abstractions. The Africa they want to be proud of needs to have a little more meat. So they sometimes personify Africa; Africa becomes embodied in a single symbolic individual. These ordinary Negroes of the New World who feel an actual spiritual need in their identification with Africa have sometimes turned to the symbolism of Ethiopia. The Emperor of Ethiopia, visiting Jamaica in April 1966, was overwhelmed by Jamaicans who thought of him as a god.

But sometimes the Negro of the New World needs a modern symbol of pride, an African leader who stands for modernity, for progress as well as for the dignity of the black man. No other African leader was as well qualified to capture the imagination of this kind of Afro-American as Nkrumah was. The black people of the United States in particular must have found it easy to identify with him: he was an ex-Harlemite, he was English-speaking, and he had a defiant pride when dealing with the government of the United States. He was a good militant symbol for radical Afro-Americanism.

This was perhaps the nearest thing to a recompense that African nationalism has paid to the Negro struggle in America. It was, as we have noted, American Negroes and West Indians who launched pan-Africanism on to a world stage. They helped to strengthen the morale of African nationalists in the colonies. But now the triumph

[25] I was present at the rally.

of African nationalism and the attainment of independence have in turn strengthened the morale of Negro fighters in the United States.

Behind it all is the influence of the liberal ethic, coupled with the feeling that those who had expounded that ethic were among the first to violate it in their dealings with the colored world. The sense of "liberalism betrayed" was, to a certain extent, what ignited African nationalism in the first place. In the words of Nnamdi Azikiwe, the spearhead of modern Nigerian nationalism:

> Having been educated in the United States, I could be expected to be steeped in the traditions of Jeffersonian democracy. But we cannot be blind to any situation which might stunt the natural development of my people towards an independent national existence. At times I am perplexed at the role of the United States on the African continent. Is this great nation buttressing the forces of European reaction so as to manacle the people of Africa and thwart their legitimate aspirations towards nationhood? [26]

III – American Origins of African Leninism

It was, in part, precisely this sense of "liberalism betrayed" which aroused African interest in Marxism. But at first the main attraction of Marxism was not as a guide to African political action but as an explanation of the actions of the imperial powers. Since independence seemed to be a distant goal, that part of Marxism which had faith in a proletarian control of the state seemed remote. There was not as yet even a proletariat in Africa. But there was one thing in Marxism which was particularly appealing to Africans: it rejected the claim to altruistic motivation which the imperial powers had made to legitimize themselves in the colonies. Perhaps nothing was better for African morale than the Marxist argument that Africa was colonized not because it was primitive but because it might be rich. The assertion that the ultimate motivation of imperial expansion was not to civilize but to exploit was the most important contribution that Marx and Lenin made to Africa's sense of her own dignity.

Yet the curious thing is that the most important school of African Leninism had, to a certain extent, its origins in the United States and came to be intimately linked to a particular African

[26] From an address delivered in Washington, D.C., on December 27, 1949. See *Zik.* . . , p. 8.

conception of what the American Revolution was all about. That school is still the one which was associated with Kwame Nkrumah for so long. For more than a decade Nkrumah exerted a significant ideological influence on an important segment of African opinion throughout the continent. Nkrumah himself was later discredited. But his fall from power is not to be mistaken for an evaporation of his ideological influence. The second generation of African radicals continue to use many of the arguments that Nkrumah contributed to the vocabulary of African political discourse.

But what are Nkrumah's links with Lenin? And in what way is this connected with the United States?

We might begin by noting that Nkrumah's first important publication twenty years ago was inspired by Lenin's theory of imperialism. It was entitled *Towards Colonial Freedom*. Nkrumah's last important publication while he was still in office was *Neo-Colonialism: The Last Stage of Imperialism*. That too owes its doctrinal inspiration to Lenin's theory of imperialism.

There is little doubt that Nkrumah quite consciously saw himself as an African Lenin. He wanted to go down in history as a major political theorist and wanted a particular stream of thought to bear his own name. Hence the term *Nkrumahism*—a name for an ideology that he hoped would assume the same historic and revolutionary status as *Leninism*. The fountainhead of both Nkrumahism and Leninism was to remain Marxism, but these two streams that flowed from Marx were to have a historic significance in their own right.

Like Lenin, Nkrumah created "the Circle," a group of friends to discuss ideas and formulate theories of revolution. Like Lenin, Nkrumah encouraged the emergence of a Marxist newspaper called *The Spark*. It is true that *The Spark* came to be more purist in its Marxism than Nkrumah himself. Nevertheless, the idea of such a newspaper was directly inspired by *Iskra* (Spark), the Marxist paper which was founded in 1901 through Lenin's initiative.

But although aspects of Marxism were present in his thought from quite early in his life, Nkrumah did not really become a Marxist-Socialist in a comprehensive sense until much later in his life. Nor would it be strictly true to regard his brand of socialism as something distinct from Leninism but sharing a common fountainhead in Marx. If anything, Nkrumahism came to be a school of Leninism. And because of the ideological influence of Nkrumah himself in Africa, Nkrumahism was, to all intents and purposes, the most important school of African Leninist thought.[27]

But what is the place of the United States in all this? To begin with, there is the simple fact that Marxism first had its impact on Nkrumah when he was in the United States as a student. He befriended C. L. R. James, a Trotskyite, and through him Nkrumah learned how an underground movement in a hostile country works. Nkrumah also acquainted himself with a diverse number of political organizations in the United States, of which the bulk were either socialist or radical-liberal.

It was also in the United States that Nkrumah was first seriously exposed to Marxist and other militant writings. He read Hegel, Marx, Engels, Lenin, and Mazzini. Nkrumah tells us in his autobiography that

> The writings of these men did much to influence me in my revolutionary ideas and activities, and Karl Marx and Lenin particularly impressed me as I felt sure that their philosophy was capable of solving these problems [of imperialism in Africa].[28]

But we soon find out in the autobiography that the book which "did more than any other" to "fire" Nkrumah's enthusiasm was neither the *Communist Manifesto* nor Lenin's *State and Revolution* but *Philosophy and Opinions of Marcus Garvey,* published in 1923. And the Garveyite movement was a product of conditions in the United States. In other words, the equalitarian appeal that Marxism had for Nkrumah was inspired by the quest for *racial* equality. Perhaps for a while Nkrumah's own developing ideology was the hybrid of Garveyite Marxism. And behind the hybrid system of thought was that old Negro indignation with "liberalism betrayed."

Another aspect of the United States which might have prepared Nkrumah for Marxism was the American myth of a classless society. This myth, coupled with that other American myth of anti-imperialism, tended to create a receptivity in foreign students towards similar ideals expressed in Marxist thought. James Coleman tells us about this early impact of American myths on foreigners studying in the United States:

[27] Some of these same points are also raised in my article "Nkrumah: the Leninist Czar," *Transition,* No. 26 (Kampala: 1966).
[28] *Ghana, the Autobiography of Kwame Nkrumah* (reprint; Edinburgh: Thomas Nelson, 1961), pp. 36-37.

Certain features of American culture—the lack of class consciousness; the heterogeneity and mobility of the population; the anti-imperialist tradition; the dynamic and competitive nature of political, social, and economic behavior—were unsettling and highly contagious influences which undoubtedly had a profound impact upon African students.[29]

American liberalism, unlike British liberalism, has always had a pronounced anticlass component. To that extent American liberalism has, curiously enough, been closer to Marxism than its British counterpart has been. This is curious particularly because the American class structure—and it does, of course, exist—is nearer to a Marxian conception of classes than is the British class structure. American classes are basically economic classes; stratification in Britain, however, is compounded by ascription, regionalism, and even such intangibles as accents of speech. British stratification does not fall as neatly into a Marxian analysis as the American structure does.

However, it is the American ethic rather than the British that is anticlass. Indeed, many Americans actually believe that they have already achieved a classless society. They have tended to confuse the absence of a nobility with an absence of classes altogether. And the myth that America is already classless has served at least one function: it has given the United States a society with only a limited class-consciousness.

The anticlass component of American liberalism could be a useful ideological preparation for Marxism in some cases. Perhaps American liberalism has too strong a hold over most Americans ever to lead to a broad acceptance of Marxism. But on non-Americans, as on highly dissatisfied Americans, its impact might be enough to lead to other ideological marriages. It had this effect on W. E. B. DuBois, the most pan-African of all American Negroes and among the most Marxist. It might well have had the same effect on Kwame Nkrumah.

But perhaps the most important meeting point between African Leninism and the American Revolution lies in pan-Africanism itself and in the general rationale for it. And the rationale is in turn intimately connected with a specific theory of imperialism and economic manipulation. A useful approach to this new aspect of the subject is by first analyzing the Leninist influence on Nkrumah

[29] *Nigeria: Background to Nationalism,* p. 244.

on this question of imperial motivation, then by studying the links of this theory with pan-Africanism and with the influence of America.

IV – Leninism and the Federal Convention

In Lenin and in Marxist thought since Lenin, *imperialism* has had a special meaning. The term includes within it the behavior of monopolistic corporations within the metropolitan countries, the domination of financiers over external relations, as well as colonial policy in the narrow sense.

In Leninist terms the paramount motivation behind the old imperial expansion was, as we have indicated, the economic exploitation of the countries which were annexed. All arguments about spreading Christianity and Western civilization or ending the Arab slave trade were merely a camouflage of the imperial profit motive.[30]

In his first book, *Towards Colonial Freedom*, Nkrumah embraced this Leninist thesis. He argued:

> The imperialist powers need the raw materials and cheap native labour of the colonies for their own capitalist industries. . . . The problem of land ownership in the colonies has risen because the colonial powers have legally or illegally seized valuable mining and plantation rights. The British are more careful than other imperialists to legitimise their seizure, but even their semi-legal methods do not disguise the fact that they have no right to rob the native of his birthright.[31]

The doctrine was comfortably consistent with the central Marxist doctrine of economic determinism. At least when simplified, economic determinism was a claim that the ultimate basis of social behavior and distribution of power lay in the realm of economics. Within Britain itself all the paraphernalia of liberal democracy was a legitimation and safeguard of the economic power enjoyed by the middle and upper classes. Major changes in history within a single society, and internationally, were always a response to changes in economic relationships and modes of production. As for

---

[30] Some of the points discussed here overlap with those in my article "Nkrumah: the Leninist Czar."

[31] *Towards Colonial Freedom* (London: William Heinemann, Limited, 1946, 1960).

imperial motivation, it was not British patriotism which wanted to have an empire; it was, in the final analysis, British capitalism.

Yet, as he got more involved in the nationalist movement, Nkrumah retreated in a significant way from economic determinism. He embraced instead a doctrine of the primacy of politics. In his own immortal words, "Seek ye first the political kingdom and all things will be added to it." It was no longer economic power that determined political relationships. On the contrary, Nkrumah came to argue that "political power is the inescapable prerequisite to economic and social power." [32] For an anticolonial nationalist such a reversal of cause and effect made sense. After all, the first task was to win political independence.

But was not Nkrumah reconverted to economic determinism when he saw that "political independence is but a façade if economic freedom is not possible also"? [33] This is arguable. The African attainment of sovereignty, when not accompanied by a change in economic relationships, gave rise to what Nkrumah called *client states*. The whole doctrine of neocolonialism seemed to reassert afresh the proposition that real power lies, in the ultimate analysis, with those who are economically powerful. Had Nkrumah been proved wrong in his old optimism of "Seek ye first the political kingdom and all things will be added to it"? Had he now stumbled on to the fact that the "political kingdom" on its own lacked the power to "add things" to itself?

Nkrumah's *Neo-Colonialism: The Last Stage of Imperialism* is an attempt to resolve this difficulty. The title of the book is, of course, more than a conscious echo of Lenin's work on *Imperialism: The Last Stage of Capitalism*.[34] Just as Lenin had tried to carry Marx's analysis of capitalism a stage further, so Nkrumah attempted to carry Lenin's analysis of imperialism a level higher. Nkrumah argues that colonialism of the old style was mitigated in its effects by its own doctrine of public accountability. There was such a thing as responsible imperialism. The new phenomenon of neocolonialism, however, lacked this inner constraint of accountability. Neocolonialism was therefore the most irresponsible form of imperialism.

---

[32] *I Speak of Freedom*, p. 162. See also Herbert J. Spiro, ed., *Africa: The Primacy of Politics* (New York: Random House, Inc., 1966).

[33] *I Speak of Freedom*, p. 44.

[34] Lenin's thesis owes a good deal to J. A. Hobson's *Imperialism: A Study* (London: G. Allen & Unwin Ltd, 1902, 1938).

For those who practise [neo-colonialism], it means power without responsibility and for those who suffer from it, it means exploitation without redress. In the days of old-fashioned colonialism, the imperial power had at least to explain and justify at home the actions it was taking abroad. In the colony those who served the ruling imperial power could at least look to its protection against any violent move by their opponents. With neo-colonialism neither is the case.[35]

A major difference between Lenin's theory and Nkrumah's lies perhaps in what each was trying to explain. Lenin's main interest was in conditions in the imperial countries themselves, Nkrumah's in conditions in the former colonies. Lenin was keen to understand what there was in Britain itself which made Britain want to dominate others. Nkrumah, on the other hand, has been more concerned to explain what factors generally continue to keep Africa in a state of being dominated. There is considerable overlap between the two theoretical preoccupations, but their centers of interest are decidedly divergent.

To a certain extent, Lenin was using imperialism as an explanation of why there had not been a proletarian revolution in the Western industrialized countries. Marx had predicted that the poor in the industrialized countries would get poorer and the rich richer, until the point of revolutionary explosion was reached. Yet it became increasingly clear that the poor of the Western countries, far from getting poorer, were actually improving their standards of living at a significant rate. Why had the Western poor betrayed their destiny of a worsening plight?

The answer lay in imperialism. The exploitation of the British Empire saved the British worker at home from total poverty and helped to save Britain from a proletarian revolution. Benjamin Disraeli's concept of the "two nations" of Britain was, in a sense, Marxian. The British people were polarizing into two potentially antagonistic "nations within the nation"—the poor versus the rich. What prevented the clash? For Lenin it was imperial expansion. The two nations of Disraeli were saved from an ultimate confrontation by the diversion of the British Empire. Lenin quotes Cecil Rhodes himself, that militant embodiment of the imperial ethic. In 1895 Rhodes had defended British imperial expansion in the following terms:

[35] Nkrumah, *Neo-Colonialism: The Last Stage of Imperialism* (London: Nelson, 1965), p. xi.

In order to save the 40 million inhabitants of the United Kingdom from a bloody civil war, we colonial statesmen must acquire new lands to settle surplus population, to provide new markets for the goods produced by them in the factories and mines. The Empire, as I have always said, is a bread and butter question. If you want to avoid civil war, you must become imperialists.[36]

But now that the Empire has disintegrated, is Britain about to have a civil war? This is where Nkrumah's theory of neocolonialism takes over. The new phenomenon of exploiting other people abroad without actually ruling them is, to a certain extent, serving the same purpose as the old imperialism of Cecil Rhodes: it is delaying the ultimate class confrontation within the metropolitan countries themselves. In the words of Nkrumah, only when neo-colonialism in turn comes to an end will "the monopolists" in the metropolitan countries "come face to face with their working class in their own countries, and a new struggle will arise within which the liquidation and collapse of imperialism will be complete." [37]

All this sounds as if Nkrumah has now been converted to the view that "the political kingdom" on its own is a poor substitute for "the commanding heights of the economy." Yet, in an important sense, Nkrumah has never really retreated from a doctrine of the primacy of politics. When he said "Seek ye first the political kingdom," he does not seem to have meant the Ghanaian kingdom on its own. In the context of his political philosophy as a whole, the real political kingdom for Africa is the kingdom of Africa itself. In his words, "The Independence of Ghana is meaningless unless it is linked up with the total liberation of the African continent." [38]

It is noteworthy that at least one school of Leninism argued virtually to the effect that a socialist revolution in the Soviet Union was meaningless unless it was linked up to the total liberation of the proletarian masses all over the world. In the words of Leon Trotsky in 1924:

The permanent revolution, in an exact translation, is the continuous revolution, the uninterrupted revolution. . . . This applies to the

[36] Lenin, in his *Imperialism: The Highest Stage of Capitalism* (1917), quotes Rhodes with relish.

[37] *Neo-Colonialism, op. cit.*, p. 256.

[38] See Stephen Dzirasa, *Political Thought of Dr. Kwame Nkrumah* (Accra: Guinea Press, n.d.), p. 14.

conquests of the revolution inside of a country as well as to its extension over the international arena.

> For Russia . . . what we need is not the bourgeois republic as a political crowning, nor even the democratic dictatorship of the proletariat and peasantry, but the workers' government supporting itself upon the peasantry and opening up the era of the international socialist revolution.[39]

Nkrumah's perspective is not as global. But if he does not believe in a "permanent revolution," he does at least believe in a kind of continuous independence movement in the African continent until Africa as a whole, including South Africa, is rescued from racialism and colonial rule.

Yet if Nkrumah believes merely in the independence of each constituent unit, he cannot complain of neocolonialism after independence and still believe in the primacy of politics. A balkanized Africa remains to him vulnerable to the danger of being manipulated by outsiders. This is not because political independence is useless without economic power; it is more because political independence is weak without political unity. Nkrumah has retained his belief in the paramountcy of politics, but there is more to politics than political freedom. Indeed, even political freedom needs a political foundation other than itself. In the African continent it needs total political union.

When political freedom is thus combined with and reinforced by political union, Africa will then be able to break the economic power that others have over her. In his new book Nkrumah argues that the exploitation of Africa is itself carried out on a pan-African basis. This is economic pan-Africanism on the part of the exploiters. Only political pan-Africanism on the part of the exploited can break the hold of the continental monopolists. According to Nkrumah,

> The foreign firms who exploit our resources long ago saw the strength to be gained from acting on a Pan-African scale. By means of interlocking directorships, cross-share holdings and other devices, groups of apparently different companies have formed, in fact, one enormous

---

[39] Trotsky, *The New Course* (1924). Stalin later adopted the parochial policy of "socialism in one country"—consolidating the Russian Revolution rather than trying to force the pace of revolution throughout the world. Will Nkrumah's successors in Ghana adopt the policy of "nationalism in one country" as distinct from pan-African adventures?

capitalist monopoly. The only effective way to challenge this economic empire and to recover possession of our heritage is for us also to act on a Pan-African basis, through a Union Government.[40]

How much of Leninism is there in Nkrumah's concept of African unity? In a sense, Nkrumah's whole idea of continental unity is an extension of the Leninist principle of organization. There is, in any case, an intimate logical connection between the idea of *organization* and the idea of *unity*. And Nkrumah grasped this interconnection when he made affirmations such as this: "Without organisational strength we are weak; unity is the dynamic force behind any great venture." [41]

He seemed to believe right up to his fall from power that an Africa disunited was, in a fundamental sense, an Africa disorganized.

But in what way is this connected with the United States? The American influence on pan-Africanism after independence had a hemispheric dimension. It was partly affected by the example of what the United States could do to a divided Latin America. But it was also affected by what the United States had achieved by uniting herself in the first place. The fear of becoming a manipulated Latin America became more pronounced when the concept of neocolonialism assumed extra importance in the vocabulary of African nationalism. But the admiration of the United States as an example of continental unity is of longer standing. It is true that for an example of how political and industrial strength can be achieved through broad planning and social discipline, African nationalists have tended to look to the Soviet Union. But for an example of how such strength can be acquired through continental unification, African nationalists have more often looked to the United States.

In the view of Nkrumah, what the Africans wished to emulate most from the American experience was the realism of the Federal Convention of Philadelphia which created a strong union in the eighteenth century. The Founding Fathers had, according to him, recognized that "though individual colonies had established their independence . . . they could not really be independent unless they were politically and economically united." And when in November 1958 Nkrumah and Sekou Touré announced their plans for the formation of a Ghana-Guinea union, they acknowledged their

[40] *Neo-Colonialism, op. cit.,* p. 259.
[41] *I Speak of Freedom,* p. 3.

admiration of the original thirteen colonies of the United States.[42]
Later on, as nonalignment became more doctrinaire, there were
inhibitions on being too open an admirer of the United States.
Sometimes the admiration of a united America was coupled with a
eulogy of the Union of Soviet Socialist Republics. Nkrumah was
then perhaps at his most comfortable in combining his enthusiasm
for the American Founding Fathers with his admiration of Russian
achievements. As Stephen Dzirasa put it in his account of Nkrumah's political thought,

> Both the United States and Russia today once existed in a terrible
> state of fragmentation. . . . But when after the War of Independence
> the several states of America decided in the interest of their future to
> close their ranks, a new political state came into being in the 18th
> century, the United States of America. Today the U.S.A. is one of the
> greatest powers in the world. Before the Russian Revolution there
> was very little that the petty kingdoms [sic] which now form the
> U.S.S.R. could boast of. Today in less than 50 years of its birth the
> Soviet Union has been able to evolve a social system of its own and
> now exercises one of the greatest influences in world politics and in
> the field of science and technology.[43]

Dzirasa goes on to add that both examples "are a great source of
inspiration which more and more convince Nkrumah that the
benefits of a political union of Africa will be immense to Africans
themselves in particular and to the rest of mankind." [44]

To a certain extent, balancing an admiration of the United
States with an admiration of the Soviet Union was indeed dictated
by considerations of nonalignment. But at least as important was
the ambivalence of Nkrumah's own ideological experience. His
response to Marxism under the stimulus of American liberalism had
long-term intellectual consequences.

But on the specific issue of voluntary renunciation of sovereignty,
the thirteen American colonies remain more relevant for pan-
Africanism than the empire created by the Russian Czars. Many an
African nationalist has looked to the United States with its wealth
and power, and then dreamed of a United States of Africa. Indeed,
the very name *United States of Africa* has often been used with

[42] See *New York Times,* November 24 and 25, 1958, May 2 and 3, 1959. See
also Colin Legum, *Pan-Africanism;* Nkrumah's speech on the inspiration of the
American colonies in *Ghana Today,* V, No. 21 (Dec. 6, 1961).
[43] *Political Thought of Dr. Kwame Nkrumah,* p. 38.
[44] *Ibid.*

the conscious intention to echo the name of the American Union and thus to conjure up an image of global stature and strength. It is true that Nkrumah had in his London days once preferred the name *Union of West African Socialist Republics*. But when Ghana and Guinea formed a union, and were later joined by Mali, the nomenclature echoed the American experiment. The charter of the Ghana-Guinea-Mali union described itself as the "nucleus of the United States of Africa." [45]

As for African discussions and arguments on the form which African unity should take, these are sometimes soaked in the language of federalism which is perhaps America's most distinctive contribution to political and constitutional thought.[46]

This takes us back to the issue of liberalism. After all, federalism was, in its genesis, intimately related to liberal values. The liberal commitment to diversity, to limited government and, especially in America, to the device of "checks and balances" found comfortable accommodation in federalist assumptions and intentions. Yet for Africa the liberal postulates of federalism are not the primary concern. African nationalists have admired the American union not for the extent to which the federal government was weakened in a system of checks and balances, but for the extent to which the subcontinent was strengthened for having united in the first place.

In the background, however, there has been a growing African consciousness of the fate of Latin America. At first it was a simple case of noting that South America had been sadly left behind in technological change by North America. As M. F. Dei-Anang, an eminent Ghanaian diplomat under Nkrumah, once put it, one had only to compare the level of development attained by the United States and that attained by the South American republics to realize "the immense advantages of a political union on a continental scale." [47] But as the Leninist theory of imperialism was transformed into a general theory of neocolonialism, Latin America ceased to be a case simply of retarded technological change. Nkru-

[45] See also Dennis Austin, *Politics in Ghana, 1946-1960*, (London: Oxford University Press, 1964), pp. 396, 398.

[46] See Nkrumah, *Africa Must Unite* (London: William Heinemann, Limited, 1963). See also Nnamdi Azikiwe, *The Future of Pan-Africanism*, an address by the Governor-General of the Federation of Nigeria in London, August 1961, published by the Nigeria High Commission. Consult also the appendices in Colin Legum's *Pan-Africanism*.

[47] Speech at the Israeli Centre, Accra, "Developments in Africa and the Place of Ghana in Them," in *Ghana Today*, VI, No. 3 (April 11, 1962).

mah warned his fellow Africans at the Addis Ababa Conference which created the Organization of African States: "We have already reached a stage where we must unite or sink into that condition which has made Latin America the unwilling and distressed prey of imperialism." [48]

The United States thus became a paradoxical symbol of two things. The best example of neocolonialism at work was what the United States was doing to Latin America; the best defense against neocolonialism was the strength that the United States gave herself at the Federal Convention in Philadelphia in 1787. Behind it all was the African fear of economic manipulation as derived from Leninist thought.

V – *Towards a Domestic African Ideology*

But liberalism and socialism have not exerted their influence only on African conceptions of their relations with others. What is now emerging is the influence of these two bodies of thought on the new social relations within the African countries themselves and the economic systems they devise. As the colonial era approached its end, socialism for the African became more than just a dose of Leninism. It ceased to be merely a theory to explain imperialism and was gradually regarded as a possible guide to concrete domestic policy after independence. To put it in another way, socialism ceased to be merely a consolation or a substitute for "liberalism betrayed" and assumed an independent respectability in its own right. On these aspects of our subject it might be pertinent to turn now from West to East Africa. Quite apart from the fact that the internal experiments of Nkrumah's Ghana have now been substantially reversed by his successors, it is possible that independent East Africa offers in any case more novel innovations in ideology and practice than independent West Africa. East Africa is also a more straightforward case of socialism coming after the liberal impact.

We might therefore begin by noting once again the paradoxical proposition that nationalism in Africa derived its original intellectual stimulation from an ethic of individualism. Now we must ask: What is individualism?

---

[48] "United We Stand," address at the Conference of African Heads of State and Government in Addis Ababa, May 24, 1963.

For the African the sense of *individualism* which mattered was not really the freedom of the individual, in spite of the rhetoric. It was more often equality between one individual and another. Unlike the term *freedom,* the word *equality* implies more than one person. Logically, one can be free of everyone else, but one can only be equal to somebody else. We might therefore say that equality is a less self-centered principle than freedom. Western individualism, being libertarian, was more self-centered than the egalitarian individualism which inspired African assertiveness. Africans aspired to bring about a world in which no African individual counted for less than an individual of another race. And while they were struggling for that world, African nationalists before independence tried to make sure that no individual African counted for more than another African either.

But what has happened since independence? The ideal of maintaining equality between Africans themselves in a given country has sometimes come into conflict with the ideal of creating equality between Africans and others. The ideal of equality between Africans presumably dictates a policy of trying to prevent the emergence of an African bourgeoisie. But in East African conditions such a policy could mean leaving the profits of the private sector of the economy to be acquired exclusively by nonindigenous entrepreneurs. Africans in Kenya might then remain equal in poverty between themselves, while the inequalities of income between them on one side and the Asians and Europeans on the other are allowed to persist.

The government of Kenya seems to have rejected, for the time being, this solution. In April 1965 the then Minister for Commerce and Industry urged non-African businessmen to identify themselves with African aspirations by inviting Africans to buy shares in their enterprises. Minister Kiano said, "While we do not discriminate against non-Africans in Kenya, the spirit of give and take should prevail." [49]

The Kenya Government Sessional Paper on African Socialism of that same year also expressed a bias for such a policy.[50] It appeared that the Kenya government was not urging African socialism so much as the Africanization of capitalism. And yet for many Kenyans—as indeed many Africans elsewhere as well—African

[49] *Uganda Argus,* April 28, 1965.
[50] *African Socialism and Its Application to Planning in Kenya* (Nairobi: Government Printers, 1965).

socialism includes the Africanization of the rudimentary capitalism which has already emerged. There is certainly a keenness in East Africa for greater African participation in commerce. But is this "equality"? Kenya's Minister for Commerce and Industry described it as a process of narrowing "the wide gap between Africans and non-Africans in commerce and trade." In Uganda Dr. Milton Obote has made similar appeals to non-African businessmen—that they should try to get more and more African shareholders. But while the gap between black East Africans and nonindigenous East Africans is being narrowed, new gaps between black East Africans themselves might be created.

The Marxist purists might argue that this is not socialism. That might be so. But it does not prevent it from being good Marxism. It was Engels who once said, "A bourgeoisie is . . . as necessary a precondition of the socialist revolution as the proletariat itself." [51] By extension one might argue that an African bourgeoisie is as necessary a precondition of an African socialist revolution as is an African proletariat. In urging the Africanization of Kenya's nascent capitalism, Kenya's Minister for Commerce and Industry might indeed have been a bad socialist, but he might still have been a good Marxist.

But the significant thing about socialistic thought in East Africa is not in its relationship to Marxism. It is not even in what is expounded in a document. It is in what seems to be taken for granted. In an ethnically pluralistic society the first task of socialism, according to this school, is not to abolish class distinctions altogether but to prevent class distinctions from coinciding with racial differences. The problems of class distinctions can be mitigated by social mobility. A person can move from one class to another. The very creation of an African bourgeoisie would be proof that social mobility can be engineered or manipulated by government policy. But while it is possible for an individual to change his class, it is not very easy for any one generation to change its race. "Racial mobility" is not entirely impossible, but it usually involves generations of mixed marriages.

If, then, racial differences are more rigid than class differences, the first precondition of social harmony in a pluralistic society is a racial diversification of the middle class. The most decisive internal revolutions which have taken place in Africa south of the Sahara

[51] "Russia and the Social Revolution," *Volksstaat* (Leipzig), April 21, 1875.

in the last few years are the overthrow of the Tutsi in Rwanda and the overthrow of the Sultan's regime in Zanzibar. In neither case was the revolution initially directed against the idea of class distinctions as such. Both Rwanda and Zanzibar had revolutions primarily because their middle and upper classes were not ethnically diversified to a sufficient degree.

Would it have been more socialistic to have thwarted those revolutions? Perhaps not. But in both Rwanda and Zanzibar ethnic minorities held political power out of proportion to their numbers. In Kenya and Uganda, however, political control had already passed to Africans. With that control goes the responsibility to prevent, among other things, the victimization of non-African minorities. Why not take over the Asian shops? Partly because opportunities for Asians in other sectors of national life were already narrowing. The Africanization of the civil service especially was inevitably accomplished at a cost to the immigrant races. To prevent the Asians from engaging in commerce as well might reduce them to a painful redundancy in the life of the country of their adoption.

But why not nationalize Asian businesses and still use Asians as government employees in those enterprises? Partly because once a business becomes a government enterprise, recruitment for it might become subject to all the usual pressures of political patronage. An Asian competing for a job in a government enterprise might well be at a greater handicap than if he had been allowed to compete with Africans in private enterprise. There is therefore a sense of social justice in plural African societies which could be best served by attempting to Africanize capitalism through the competitive methods of capitalism itself. Because the government is engineering the whole competition, this is not laissez-faire capitalism. Yet it is not state capitalism either. It is the paradox of state-induced free competition between races. The fact that the new African entrepreneur gets special government encouragement does not negate the fairness of the competition. The immigrant communities have had a head start in business enterprise. Only special government assistance to Africans could counterbalance that start and help to equalize business opportunities between the races.

But will the governments of East and Central Africa limit themselves to this? Kenya's Tom Mboya has asserted that any move to buy up all Asian shops and install Africans "would hardly be a progressive action."[52] The ambition for the time being remains that of racially diversifying the bourgeoisie rather than keeping out the Asians from that class altogether in the days ahead. Given that the ultimate equality which matters to African nationalists is equality between races rather than between classes, the diversification of the bourgeoisie can to many Africans be defended in intelligible socialistic terms. But there are temptations in the situation which might make African governments more overtly racialistic against immigrant races in the future. If that happens, Africans would be betraying even their own brand of socialistic egalitarianism.

What about a tribal diversification of the African elite? In terms of education, African elites are already tribally diversified to a significant extent. But in terms of equalizing opportunities after independence, tribal nepotism is rampant in many parts of the continent.

Is tribal nepotism worse in multiparty countries like the old Nigeria and Uganda than in single-party countries? Probably only marginally worse, and then only because a multiparty system gives nepotism a chance to masquerade as something more respectable. It permits nepotism to disguise itself as normal political patronage for party supporters.

Countries like Ghana under Nkrumah and Tanzania under Nyerere linked their socialism to the ethic of a one-party structure. And the socialistic one-party state was then viewed as the instrument for integrating tribes into a nation. Indeed, even in countries without a one-party structure a hankering for such a structure is sometimes betrayed at the highest level. The ruling party in Uganda, the Uganda People's Congress, made no secret of its desire to see the other parties dissolve themselves. In fact, there is a good deal of evidence to suggest that one of the attractions of socialism in Africa after independence lies in its association with centralized government. A socialistic government is then definable as a government which is, or aspires to be, a centralizing agent, one which subjects the economy to state manipulation and subjects the tribes to national integration.

This is a significant departure from the ethic of individualistic liberalism which, as we noted at the beginning, provided the initial

[52] *Uganda Argus,* December 15, 1964.

impetus to African nationalistic assertion. After independence the slogan becomes, at best, "one man, one vote—one party." In fact, the addendum of "one party" becomes politically more significant than the original principle of "one man, one vote." The liberal rhetoric of "freedom of the individual" becomes less evident in speeches. Socialistic ideals of "the task of development" and the elimination of "factionalism" assume a kind of ommipresence. Even in countries which, in practice, are out to create an African bourgeoisie you will hear the doctrine of "African classlessness" glorified. Here again one must not be misled by the language of African politics. When you take a closer look at the gap between political language and concrete political behavior you might find that the glorification of classlessness is merely another way of articulating a fear of factionalism and a desire for national integration. In East Africa the rhetoric of classlessness is therefore compatible with the integrative function which would be served by an ethnic diversification of the middle classes. And behind it all is, hopefully, a government with a socialistic capacity for central manipulation.

Africa has borrowed a good deal of theory from the intellectual tradition of Western politics and from Leninist theories of expansionism. But the uses to which Africa has put these ideas bear a stamp of practical originality. African nationalists first subscribed to liberal values of individualism and free speech as they carried on the struggle against colonialism. Socialistic values of development and centralism then became the goals of many African governments after independence. Liberalism, coupled with some Leninist language, served the cause of Africa's political emancipation. Socialism as an internal structure is now being made to serve the cause of Africa's economic liberation.

In some ways it is fitting that history should have played the ideological game this way. There is indeed something rather disintegrative about liberal values; thus the weapon which was needed to fight Western empires was an ethic of disintegration. And so empires dissolved by a progressive application of individualistic norms like "one man, one vote." But after independence the task becomes that of domestic integration in each liberated unit. For this purpose the old individualistic values which fought against colonialism now begin to be qualified, and centralizing socialistic norms gain ascendancy.

A special attempt at synthesizing the two value systems lies in the Tanzanian experiment. With her first general elections since independence, Tanzania embarked on a constitutional novelty in 1965. Members of TANU contested the same seats with each other. Several ministers lost their seats, including the Minister of Finance.[53] To some extent the elections vindicated the original idea of setting up a Presidential Commission to investigate how liberal democratic values could best be safeguarded under a one-party system. The elections were also a kind of ideological triumph for Julius Nyerere himself. In his pamphlet *Democracy and the Party System* of 1962, Nyerere attempted a theoretical marriage between the one-party idea and the ethic of individualism. He argued that a two-party system could all too easily stifle individualism through its party discipline. And the rationale for the discipline was the fear which each party had of giving advantage to the opposition. By contrast, a one-party situation constituted "an opportunity to dispense with the disciplines of the Two-Party system." Nyerere argued that the Westminster model in a situation like that of Tanganyika actually militated against individual freedom. He himself looked forward to the day when TANU members would be as free from the rigidities of party discipline in Parliament as they already were at the party's own National Executive meetings.[54] And that day had to await a constitutional transformation in Tanganyika—the kind of transformation which would allow members of the party even to contest the same parliamentary seats with each other.

Yet this is the same Nyerere who regards the possibility of organized opposition to major lines of policy as a "civil war situation." [55] The same fear of factionalism which one finds in other proponents of the one-party ethic is strongly evident in Nyerere. And so Nyerere would like to see all political disputes to be joined as disputes between individuals on points of policy and not as disputes between organized groups. To prevent group formation without sacrificing individualism is perhaps what the new Tanzanian constitutional experiment is all about. It is an exercise in "individualized centralism"—promising, but also very precarious.

It is not without significance that this liberally imaginative country in East Africa is also among the most socialistic. And socialism

[53] For a brief account of the elections see Colin Legum's evaluation in *The Observer* (London), September 26, 1965.

[54] *Democracy and the Party System* (Dar es Salaam: Tanganyika Standard Limited, 1962?), pp. 4-5.

[55] This is certainly the implication of his assertion that a two-party system is either an argument about trivialities or a framework for civil war. *Ibid.*, p. 8.

to Tanzania, as to many other African countries, is attractive partly because of its purported centralizing functions. Political integration is accelerated by getting the people "involved"—and socialism is conceived of as a doctrine of mass involvement. And so, in spite of the novelty of the Tanzanian experiment, the following generalization hopefully still captures the essence of Africa's ideological experience: Out of the liberal ethic was born African *nationalism*, and now out of socialism is sought African *nationhood*. Perhaps the whole relationship between borrowed theory and original practice in African politics is ultimately reducible to this single proposition.

V

Repetition or Innovation?

Herbert J. Spiro

Publication of this book coincides with the tenth anniversary of the independence of the Gold Coast. Ghana was the first colony in Black Africa to gain independence from European rule. Under the leadership of Kwame Nkrumah—variously described as charismatic, dynamic, innovative, repressive, dictatorial, or megalomaniac— Ghana played an important role in the movement for African unity, in the activities of the "Third World," and, despite its relatively small population and "power," even in the international politics of the Cold War. But more than a year before completion of the first decade of Ghana's independence, Kwame Nkrumah was overthrown by a military *coup d'état*. One month before this event the military of the Federation of Nigeria had replaced its rather less dynamic and less innovative civil governments. Soon after the Ghanaian coup the Prime Minister of Uganda ousted the Kabaka of Buganda from the Presidency of Uganda and, subsequently, from his palace in the capital, after a fierce and reportedly bloody battle. In the Congo the head of the national army took over as President and ordered the public execution by hanging of four former ministers in Leopoldville. A number of other French-speaking countries in Black Africa were also scenes of military takeovers. Charges of corruption, nepotism, inefficiency, and repression usually preceded, accompanied, and followed these anticonstitutional, or at least extraconstitutional, happenings.

All of this has served to revive the controversy about the repetitive or innovative characteristics of African politics, perhaps more outside than inside the continent itself. The beginnings of this debate coincided roughly with Ghana's attainment of independence. The discussion probably achieved its peak in the early 1960s, when the majority of Black African colonies gained statehood and, with it, membership in the United Nations. If an opinion survey could have been taken among persons acquainted with and interested in African affairs, in which they would have been asked whether they expected Africa to repeat more or less the patterns of development that had been observed in other developing areas, or whether they expected Pliny's dictum "always something new out of Africa" to be revalidated by Africa's pattern of development, chances are that a large majority would have been found, and would still be found, on the side of repetition.

I – *The Expectation of Repetition*

We can identify at least three reasons why many observers might have expected African events to repeat earlier patterns.

First, there was the concept of *developing areas*, which was applied to Africa after it had been worked out by scholars mainly concerned with one of the older areas, especially South and Southeast Asia and the Middle East. Application of the term to Black Africa, when that area came to the attention of scholars and policymakers, suggested *a priori* that the major problems of Africa would be similar to those of the other regions and that, therefore, solutions to these problems could be best devised by way of analogy to the problems of their more successful forerunners elsewhere. The timing of Africa's move to the center of the world stage was of importance in this connection, because the occasionally excessive optimism with which many had looked forward to the full independence of colonies like India or protectorates like Egypt had by the late 1950s been disappointed and, in some instances, had been turned into an equally excessive pessimism about the latest developing area, Africa.

Moreover, as Professor Friedrich points out, many societies in the regions whose "emergence" had been noticed earlier had old and in some cases quite ancient cultures, which were expected to provide foundations or frameworks for their modern development. With the possible exception of Ethiopia, no society in sub-Saharan Africa could match the cultural "capital" with which India and Pakistan emerged into independence. But even India and especially Pakistan were undergoing severe crises of development. Did this not warrant the expectation of worse things for Black Africa? Again, comparison of the "infrastructure" left behind by the departing colonial powers in the older developing areas and in Africa showed the latter to be starting out at a considerable disadvantage, partly because the scramble for Africa had started long after the Europeans had already been firmly established in countries like Indonesia or Ceylon. Another factor that was generally taken as a poor augury for Black Africa in comparison with Asia and the Middle East, and even more so with Latin America, was the much smaller proportion of the total population of persons with the kind of Western education believed to be essential for promoting development. Especially before students of development refined their concepts of social structure and class,[1] some considered the relative thinness of African equivalents of a bourgeoisie or middle class a bad omen for development. Where could the new African states find the equivalent of those groups which had provided the major impetus for the modernization of Japan, without either native bourgeoisie or aristocracy?

Of course, all of these apparent deficiencies of Africa by comparison with older developing areas need not automatically have led their discoverers to expect repetition at a lower level of performance. They might just as well have concluded that Africa would show innovation at a higher level. For example, the likelihood of weaker nationalisms in Africa than in Asia, the Middle East, and Latin America could have lent itself to a positive interpretation and prognosis, of the kind that Professor Abu-Lughod places upon it. In fact, however, many students of the developing areas who focused upon Africa either sought to play down the comparative weakness of nationalisms there or concluded that this weakness made "national integration" the primary goal and an essential prerequisite of development.

These interpretations can easily be explained by the highly normative connotation of the concept of *developing areas*, at least around the high point of the African independence movement. At that time most students of the subject assumed that the countries in these areas were obviously developing, or should be developing, toward the kind of conditions which developed nations had already achieved—especially the most highly developed ones, like the United States, the United Kingdom, or Sweden. The goals of the process of development were thus taken for granted, and, because the models were well known, the further assumption was made that the process would have to pass through the same "stages of growth,"

[1] For one such useful refinement see John H. Kautsky, "An Essay in the Politics of Development," *Political Change in Underdeveloped Countries: Nationalism and Communism* (New York: John Wiley & Sons, Inc., 1962), pp. 1-119.

in the same sequence, with analogous side effects, which had characterized the development of these mature systems. Hence the negative interpretations placed upon the absence of ancient culture, of wide and firm infrastructure, of middle class or aristocracy, and of conventional nationalism. All of these "prerequisites" of development had been present to varying degrees in the already developed areas. Their absence, as one reputable sociologist put it to me in 1960, foretold the inevitability of utter chaos in Black Africa. "I wish," he said, "we could erect a fence around the whole damned continent for the next one hundred years to permit structures to develop before we let them loose in the world." Nor was he joking.

The first explanation of majority expectaions of repetition rather than innovation thus builds upon the concept of *developing areas* itself. Specialists on development, especially if they had been disappointed once before by the performance of another area, were not going to be caught wrong again. By drawing their sample of developing systems exclusively from those areas currently believed to be engaged in the process of development, where little innovation had been taking place and less had been noticed, they tended to foreclose the possibility of innovation in Black Africa. Moreover, because Africa, judged by most of their indices of development, was more backward than the other areas, the repetition they anticipated was at a lower level of performance.

The second reason why the majority of observers expected repetition rather than innovation in Africa explains in particular the attitude toward Africa of those scholars who were critical of the concepts of *developing areas,* of *development,* or of the earlier notion of "The Non-Western Political Process." [2] Explicitly or implicitly, these scholars denied that there was some qualitative uniqueness about the politics of the developing areas and asserted that there were certain universals of politics which made possible political theory and political science. This view is represented in this book by Professor Friedrich's chapter:

Aware of the distinctive nature of the political community which they rule . . . these leaders [of developing countries] often under-

[2] See Lucian W. Pye, "The Non-Western Political Process," *The Journal of Politics,* XX, No. 3 (Aug. 1958), 468-86. See also Alfred Diamant's brilliant critique of Pye's paper, unfortunately ignored by most subsequent scholarship on the subject, "Is There a Non-Western Political Process?" *The Journal of Politics,* XXI, No. 1 (Feb. 1959), 123-27. See also my "Constitutional and Legal Aspects of Political Development," *Theory and Practice of Political Development* (Washington, D.C.: The Brookings Institution, 1967).

estimate the contribution that a truly general political science has to make to the solution of their problems. . . . So unless we base the . . . meaning [of *politics*] upon the Western pattern of development from absolutism to constitutionalism, it remains an open question just what the "development of politics" in the sense of political development means. . . . These governments [of the new countries] ought to be constitutional, but cannot be, because the prerequisites of constitutional government are lacking and will have to be developed.

When we apply these sentences to our present question about the expectation of repetition rather than innovation in the politics of Africa, three propositions emerge: (1) African leaders can learn lessons from valid generalizations upon observed political reality, present and past; (2) these lessons are drawn from the Western pattern of political development from absolutism to constitutionalism; and (3) the developing countries cannot yet achieve the goal of constitutionalism (on the Western model), because it is precisely the prerequisites of constitutional government that they lack and must first develop.

Mr. Friedrich concluded his chapter by quoting a dictum of Governor Muñoz Marin, "to govern is to invent," and he himself opts for the middle road between those who see eternal repetitions and those who would utterly disregard the experience of the past. Nevertheless, his "open question" about the meaning of "the development of politics," if this means something other than development toward the Western type of constitutionalism, suggests at the minimum that the new states in Africa and elsewhere ought to try to move in the general direction of constitutionalism as it has evolved and is still evolving in the West, and at the maximum that they will in fact be moving in that direction, presumably with the up's and down's that Western countries have experienced on this path.

Although critics of the uniqueness assumption often deny that there are specific economic, social, or cultural prerequisites of either development or "stable democracy," they more often agree with the proposition that there are certain other, presumably political prerequisites of the kind of constitutionalism to which they themselves are committed. In a sense, this makes them even more pessimistic than the development specialists about the feasibility of innovation —or more opposed in principle to qualitative political innovation. This is so because these critics speak from a deeper historical and a wider geographical perspective. When even France and Germany have repeatedly relapsed in the course of their progress toward better constitutionalism, when things go wrong even in Britain and in the United States, then one can hardly harbor very sanguine expectations of Malawi, Kenya, or Guinea.

While the first reason for expecting repetition was connected with the concept of *developing areas,* and the second with a critique of the assumption of uniqueness implied by that concept, the third reason had little directly to do with concepts or methods, flowing rather more from practical considerations of foreign policy in the Cold War. Competition between the Western and Communist powers in the Third World grew steadily in the years between the end of World War II and the year of maximum births of African states, 1960. Communist expectations of repetition were stimulated in part by such concepts of Marxist-Leninist-Maoist ideology as "national liberation wars." Similar Western expectations were, to some extent, mirror images of Soviet (and, later, Chinese) Communist anticipations, since Western policy-makers expected the Communists to pursue policies toward the developing areas that would be congruent with their ideology, and therefore often tried to preempt such moves by intervening—in supportive or other ways—before the communists did. This competition had already contributed to instability and violence in Asia, the Middle East, and Latin America, and most policy-makers tended to look toward escalation of the competition as Europe's African colonies were propelled into independence—a process that was itself accelerated by Cold War competition. At this point, many of them may also have been influenced by the literature on the developing areas and its general assumption that Black Africa was less well prepared for independence than the older regions. Indigenous "structures" and commitment to them would therefore be weaker, and even a lower degree of outside interference could be expected to produce greater disturbances than in South or Southeast Asia, the Middle East, or Latin America. African politicians who would become active in international relations, especially within the United Nations system, would have much less training and experience than their forerunners from the other developing areas; hence the anticipation of repetition at a lower level of performance. Again, however, this was not a necessary conclusion, because the Africans' freshness at international diplomacy might just as well have prompted them to innovate in a field in which old forms are often ill suited to deal with the content of new problems. Similarly, the Africans' presumable lack of ideological sophistication could have made them less interested in and less susceptible and more resistant to ideological appeals designed for Indians, Indochinese, or Arabs.

This option between expectations of repetition and innovation, which was open to those who in fact anticipated repetition in Africa, suggests that the conceptual and the political reasons are not entirely unrelated to one another. All of these attitudes and concepts were, after all, formulated in the climate of the Cold War, which created the major problems and issues of the period for politicians and social scientists alike. I would not be surprised, therefore, if it should prove possible to establish some general congruence between the points at which individual scholars can be placed on the African repetition-innovation spectrum and on the Cold War spectrum, whose corresponding right and left poles might be described as "continuing hard line confrontation" and "experimental soft line accommodation." I say this without in any way wishing to identify particular scholars as "hawks" or "doves"—good scholars are more properly classified as owls—but only in order to point to some possible intellectual affinities. I will return to this question later in the discussion of reactions to the coups in Nigeria and Ghana.

II – The Expectation of Innovation

Those who expected the new Africa to become politically innovative were probably in an over-all minority and appear to me to include more "liberals," just as the repetition-expecting majority appear to include more "conservatives." The reasons for their expectations are of equal interest. Again I discern three major ones.

First, there was an often explicit rejection of the kind of analogy upon which the expectation of repetition was based. This applied to analogies with both the other developing areas and the older national states of the West. For example, in 1964 I wrote:

[Another] comparison is between the new states of Africa and older ex-colonies on the other continents that are usually described as developing areas. . . .

First, there has been a relatively low incidence of violence, both organized police or military violence and less mob violence. Second, African politics have been less moved and motivated by ideologies and other rigid doctrines than postindependence politics in the other major developing areas. Third, African politics have displayed a more creative, less stultifying attitude toward law than the politics of the other regions, and especially those in which the traditions of Roman or Islamic law prevail. And, fourth, African politicians—again taken as a class, and at least until now—have been more flexible and adaptable than their counterparts in the other areas, without at the same time being nearly as cynical or corrupt as a Diem, a Nuri al-Said, or a Trujillo, three leaders who were murdered in part because their political style promoted political instability.[3]

And in 1961:

In contrast to conventional sovereign nation-states, the new sub-Saharan members of the international community did not come into being, nor did their leaders come to the fore, through the use of organized force on a large scale. After achieving statehood, they have been less preoccupied with questions of territorial frontiers than their older models. None of the new states has a culturally homogeneous population and none intends to differentiate the culture of its people as much as possible from the cultures of its neighbors, as other nations have been culturally differentiated, deliberately, all over the globe. The new African states, therefore, lack the military, geographical, and cultural substance of the national states with which we are familiar. By recognizing this, they may be able to avoid many of the negative experiences—international and civil war, Irrendentism, cultural chauvinism—through which most other states have passed, and are passing still, in the modern age. The new Africa may also make a positive contribution to the constitutional development of the global community of mankind.[4]

The relation between political development and modernization in the new African countries could also be anticipated to follow a pattern quite different from the European, the North American, or, as Professor Welch has shown, the Japanese models. In Japan, as previously (e.g., in Germany), modernization was pushed through by a small administrative elite, a true "ruling class," without possibility, not to speak of any encouragement, of popular participation. In Black Africa, on the other hand, popular participation emerged long before modernization in the independence movements that were subsequently reorganized into the political parties, which are only now addressing themselves to the tasks of modernization with, on the whole, only indifferent success.

[3] "Political Stability in the New African States," *The Annals of the American Academy of Political and Social Science,* vol. 354 (July 1964), 99f.
[4] *Politics in Africa: Prospects South of the Sahara* (Englewood Cliffs, N.J.: Prentice-Hall, Inc., 1962), p. v.

All of this pointed to a much more political meaning of development within the African context which, according to this interpretation, warranted talk of a peculiarly African "primacy of politics." From this point of view, political development in the sense of the development of politics did not mean repetition of the Western pattern of evolution from absolutism to constitutionalism. Nor was its meaning, for that reason, an "open question," in Professor Friedrich's phrase. Rather, it meant the growth of politics. There would be more and more politics; more people, and a larger proportion of the population, would be participating in politics, would become aware of the possibilities of politics; the volume of issues would increase; politicians (not necessarily "rulers," or "leaders," or "governors") would literally invent new goals, popularize these goals, and thereby further increase popular awareness and participation. This whole complicated process—of which only utopian optimists conceived in a unilinear onward-upward-forward way—was bound to lead to political innovation, including new constitutional forms, which could not be adequately judged by applying to them the yardstick of even the most successful Western constitutions.[5]

The second reason for expecting innovation derived from actual events in the new states during the first few years after independence. At least on the surface, a great deal of political innovation actually did take place. The issue here is not the direction in which particular institutional, procedural, or ideological devices pointed, or whether the observer found himself in sympathy or antipathy with them. (If, like most innovation-expectant analysts, he did not look upon Western constitutionalism as the ultimate achievement of man's constitutional genius, he probably sympathized with the experimental character of many of these unpatented inventions. If, like most repetition-expectant students, his criteria were conventionally Western, he was probably critical of the new gadgets and dubious about their success.) The question is only the actual incidence of political innovation, and the answer could be determined simply from the expanding—or the inflating—vocabulary of African politics: African socialism, whose content and significance Professor Mazrui has described; African one-party states, which have

---

[5] See my "New Constitutional Forms in Africa," *World Politics*, XIII, (Oct. 1960), 69-76. "The merits of a new African constitution are unrelated to the fidelity with which it copies that of the United Kingdom, the United States, or one of the last three French Republics" (p. 70).

given rise to a series of controversies[6] but which almost certainly differ from single-party regimes in other developing and developed countries; the Organization of African Unity, which, whatever its achievements or the lack thereof, has operated in ways quite different from those of other regional international organizations; the African caucus at the United Nations,[7] which introduced some novel informal procedures into that body; and the like. There was the further and related novelty after independence, anticipated by some during the "terminal colonial stage," of the peculiarly internationalist form of nationalism—if, indeed, that term is at all appropriate—which Professor Abu-Lughod has compared with its nominal counterparts in other areas of the world.

All of this was seen as innovative and, frequently, as unprecedented in form or content or both. In my own judgment, all this and much other evidence of innovation also shared in common the further distinctive characteristic of pointing in the direction of the increasing development of politics, in the sense given above. This is not meant to suggest that it pointed toward some sort of African millennium of freely and fully political utopias, but simply toward the more or less continuous expansion of politics. And here I would make a further distinction in addition to that between level and process of development made in the Introduction, which students of political development usually overlook, with confusing results. This is the distinction between quantity and quality of political development. At present we are concerned with quantitative development in Africa, which can hardly be denied: there is more politics in Black Africa in 1967 than there was in 1957, 1962, or 1965; more today than yesterday; more tomorrow than today. The quality or, as I prefer, the style of this increased volume of politics raises quite a different order of questions. Most of those who expect repetition are critical of the quality of the politics which they observe and, partly because they may also harbor a generally negative or at least ambivalent attitude toward politics as such, they therefore deny the

[6] See, for example, Martin Kilson, Jr., "Authoritarian and Single-Party Tendencies in African Politics," *World Politics,* XV, No. 2 (Jan. 1963), 262-94; Clement Henry Moore, "Mass Party Regimes in Africa" in *Africa: The Primacy of Politics,* H. J. Spiro, ed. (New York: Random House, Inc., 1966), pp. 85-115.

[7] See Thomas Hovet, Jr., *Africa in the United Nations* (Evanston, Ill.: Northwestern University Press, 1963), and the same author's "African Politics in the United Nations" in Spiro, ed., op. cit., pp. 116-49.

possibility or the reality or the desirability of both innovation and development.[8]

The third reason for the minority expectations of innovation, like the other side's counterpart of it, was again more political and less conceptual or methodological and revolved especially around the potential role to be played by the new states in the world politics of the Cold War. Even though, in this interpretation, earlier neutralists like Nehru or Nasser may have failed in their efforts to reduce the ideological and violent manifestations of that conflict, similar (but not therefore necessarily analogous) efforts by African international politicians were more likely to succeed. Moreover, the innovation-expectants wanted such efforts to succeed, whereas the repetition-expectants might have considered these attempts at best irrelevant to the great confrontation, at worst immoral. The former reasoned that international innovation could be expected for a number of reasons, among them the sheer quantity of new African states that participate in world politics, the comparatively unviolent way in which they had achieved their independence, their relative indifference to the ideological and power issues of the Cold War, their interest in reducing the tensions of that conflict so that developed states could devote greater resources to development assistance, and the the analogy between the development of politics in the new Africa and the development of world politics in the global system, which would provide opportunities for African international politicians to apply their freshly gained experience in political innovation to the rigidities of the Cold War. Here, hopes ran particularly high for reduction of the ideological content of Western-Communist relations—and hopes were just as hard to

[8] Professor Samuel P. Huntington seems to distinguish between quantitative development, which he identifies as social mobilization, and qualitative political development, i.e., the institutionalization of political organizations and procedures. Political development, in his sense of the term, should move toward democracy and stability, among other goals. He finds social mobilization in direct conflict with institutionalization. In other words, he asserts that the quantitative development of politics leads to "political decay." He therefore offers three methods for slowing down social mobilization: increasing the complexity of the social structure; limiting or reducing communications in the society; and minimizing competition among segments of the political elite. This sounds like throwing out the baby of expanded popular participation and awareness with the bathwater stability and "legitimacy." "Political Development and Decay," *World Politics*, XVII, No. 3 (April 1965), 386-430, especially 419ff.

distinguish from the expectations of the innovationists as were fears from the expectations of the repetitionists. Professor Mazrui's chapter elucidates these expectations and judges the extent to which they had been borne out by 1966.[9]

III – The Dialectic of Opposing Interpretations

To what extent have any of these early expectations, of both innovation and repetition in African politics, been confirmed or contradicted by events in the decade since the Gold Coast became Ghana? It is easier to deal with this question now, after the series of dramatic events of the first two months of 1966, and especially in the light of the military *coups d'état* in Nigeria and Ghana and the reaction of outside observers of African politics to these coups. These two takeovers lend themselves particularly well to our purpose because they involved the overthrow of such radically different regimes. They should be studied in conjunction with the reactions of outside analysts because attitudes toward the governments of Sir Abubakar in Nigeria and Dr. Nkrumah in Ghana used to pro-

[9] Senator Robert F. Kennedy expressed innovationist expectations of African international behavior in a speech delivered in Addis Ababa, Ethiopia, on June 15, 1966. After declaring that the underdeveloped world "can be the sword to cut the knot" of the nuclear deadlock, and charging that the great powers, including the United States, "are simply not doing enough . . . to arrive at an agreement," he continued:

> You must therefore assume a responsibility that others have been unable to fulfill. You must now take the lead and restore the flagging energies of governments and their negotiators. In every world capital, in governments and in every international capital, in every embassy, in every international organization, you must make it clear that you regard as true world leaders only those nations which are willing to walk the last mile, take the last step, in the search for the control of the atom. . . . Hundreds of millions of people, in my country, in the Soviet Union, in Europe and Asia and here in Africa, would die within the first 24 hours of a full-scale nuclear exchange, and as Chairman Khrushchev once said, the living would envy the dead. Even nations with no part in the conflict whatever, unaffected directly by such a war, would find themselves without markets for their goods, without assistance for their development, without the accumulated wisdom and experience of the world community. So your stake—Africa's stake—in a non-proliferation treaty is as great as that of any of the great powers.

Dispatch by Lloyd Garrison, *New York Times*, June 16, 1966, p. 7.

vide something like an acid test of one's location on the repetition-innovation spectrum. The same has turned out to be true of reactions to the coups themselves.

Those who expected innovation, in general, saw President Nkrumah as its principal prophet and engineer, both within his own country and for the continent as a whole. He had resisted British pressures toward accepting a strongly federalist terminal colonial constitution. He had replaced the actual terminal constitution with a deliberately "genuinely African" charter, which appeared to be full of novel institutions and procedures. He had pioneered, and seemed to have institutionalized, a novel kind of one-party system in his Convention People's Party, which could be looked upon as a classic example of what Professor Huntington has called the "primacy of party." [10] Nkrumah was the most prolific and one of the most articulate political theorists in Africa, as Professor Mazrui has shown. He was the leader of the centralist wing of the pan-African unity movement. He played an unusually active role in the politics of the Third World and of the Cold War, especially through the United Nations, of whose General Assembly his Foreign Minister had served as President. Nkrumah had explicitly rejected the desirability and the possibility of repeating in Africa the patterns of development through which both Western and Communist developed countries had passed. He was trying to forge his own goals rather than adopt mechanically the ready-made goals of either East or West. In short, he was an innovator and he was in power. Those who favored innovation loved him.

Those who expected repetition disliked or hated Nkrumah. They looked upon the Nkrumah constitution as window dressing for the Nkrumah dictatorship with its barely disguised "totalitarian" tendencies. His rejection of "tried and proven" Western principles of constitutional democracy and private free enterprise suggested that he was either a knave or a fool. His ideology was viewed as crypto-Communist or hogwash. His meddling in world politics, especially at the United Nations, was condemned as irresponsible at best, pro-Soviet at worst. His "new" goals were viewed as a façade for his personal pursuit of unlimited power, not in Ghana alone, but over the whole continent of Africa. If this was an instance of "new con-

[10]Huntington, *op. cit.,* p. 424. Huntington urged the United States to support regimes that have institutionalized such parties, rather than regimes with charismatic leaders or military chiefs; *ibid.,* pp. 428f.

stitutional forms," as the prognosticator of the *Death of Africa* put it, "We'll take vanilla!" [11]

The attitudes of the two extremes of the interpretative spectrum toward the old regime in the Federation of Nigeria were exactly the reverse. Those who favored repetition saw Nigeria as the "last white hope of Africa," in a manner of speaking, precisely because its leaders—especially Sir Abubakar, the Federal Prime Minister, and the Sardauna of Sokoto, the Premier of the Northern Region—had refused to innovate constitutionally. They had made an honest effort to operate the terminal colonial constitution, with all its immensely complicated federalism and English legalism.[12] They had not imposed a single-party system, at least not at the federal level. They accepted the values of Western constitutionalism (though not always of Western democracy), with an admixture of Islamic political philosophy in the Northern Region. They promoted private Nigerian and foreign investment and seemed to favor modernization over the development of politics. They were realistic rather than utopian about the prospects of political union for their continent. They conducted themselves with restraint in international relations and often seemed to lean more toward the West on issues arising out of the Cold War in the United Nations. Nigeria's chances for successful development appeared excellent precisely because its elite was evidently trying to follow the development models of other developing areas and the developed nations, while also learning from mistakes that might have been committed elsewhere.

For these same reasons, advocates of innovation tended to be very critical of postindependence Nigeria. The federal constitution, even after the formal change had been made from monarchy to republic, was too conventionally Western. Federalism tended to amplify the already existing centrifugalism of tribal and regional loyalties. The same was true of the maintenance of three major parties, each of them strongly identified with a single region. The self-proclaimed conservatism of the dominant Northern leaders was viewed as an anachronism and was expected to result in violent uprisings against the semifeudal ruling class in the Northern Region. Nigeria's iden-

---

[11] Susan and Peter Ritner, "Africanism's Constitutional Malarkey," *The New Leader* (June 10, 1963), pp. 17-21. See my reply, *The New Leader* (July 22, 1963) pp. 25f. Also Peter Ritner, *The Death of Africa* (New York: Macmillan, 1960).

[12] See F. A. O. Schwarz, Jr., *Nigeria: The Tribes, the Nation, or the Race—The Politics of Independence* (Cambridge, Mass.: M.I.T. Press, 1965).

tification with the Monrovia group of states and its leaders' preference for functional cooperation, as distinguished from political unification for all of Africa, constituted an unnecessary roadblock, the more so because Nigeria was the most populous African state. The often ostentatiously moderate behavior of the Nigerian representatives at the United Nations hindered the fight against neocolonialism. All of this put together meant not only that Nigeria's own prospects for development were judged poor, but also that its government—precisely because of its refusal to avail itself of opportunities to innovate—was retarding development elsewhere in Africa.

Only two regimes as apparently different from each other as those of Ghana and Nigeria before 1966 could have elicited such diametrically opposite attitudes from Western students of developing countries. Then both civil governments were overthrown by the military within a period of little more than one month. Again the reactions of the innovation-school and the repetition-school were diametrically opposed to each other. The innovators welcomed the overthrow of the Nigerian government and constitution, but were appalled by the overthrow of the *Osagyefo* of Ghana. The repetitionists were dismayed by the fall and murder of Sir Abubakar (even if this could be taken as definitive corroboration of their thesis, since this had been the African country voted most likely to succeed, yet it was obviously repeating a familiar Latin American or Middle Eastern or Pakistani or Burmese pattern), but pleased by the removal of Dr. Nkrumah because it brought authentic indigenous proof, they claimed, of the very charges that they had been making against him *ab initio* from the outside. They now turned on Nkrumah's Western supporters or sycophants in a way not unlike the behavior of some old-time Western anti-Stalinists toward Western students of Soviet affairs who had not been critical of Stalin, after the latter's death and Khrushchev's "secret" exposé of his viciousness. They said, in effect, "We told you so. Now we are being proven right, and our thesis about the likelihood of repetition is being confirmed."

At this point one fact becomes interesting. While the reactions of outsiders to the two coups differed so radically, the motives and objectives of the two inside groups of military *putschists,* and their operating procedures after they came into power, were rather similar despite the radical differences between the two regimes they had overthrown. Both groups of army officers, later supported by the

police and the professional civil servants, were opposed to inefficiency, corruption, and the slow rate of economic modernization,
even though these maladies took different forms in Nigeria and
Ghana. In Nigeria, they appeared as a manifestation of the plethora
of politics; in Ghana, as a manifestation of the dearth of politics.

Now, there is nothing peculiarly African about the advocacy of
efficiency, honesty, and quick economic progress by professional military men in developing or developed countries. But there do seem
to be two additional features which characterized the new military
rulers of both Nigeria and Ghana and at the same time distinguished them from their counterparts in other regions, both developing and developed. First, both groups of officers conducted
themselves in remarkably "civil" ways. They not only used a minimum of violence in both cases, but in Nigeria the assassins themselves were not permitted to run the show after the initial overthrow, and in Ghana the coup was deliberately scheduled to
coincide with President Nkrumah's absence, to minimize bloodshed.
After the takeovers the usual marks of military rule—roadblocks,
armed troops in urban centers, large-scale arrests, executions, establishment of detention camps—were little in evidence.

Second, neither military junta declared itself opposed to politics
as such—as most military juntas in Latin America, Asia, the Middle
East, and, for that matter, in Europe have usually done. To be
sure, the Nigerian military government declared its opposition to
the political excesses of the regime to whose life it had literally put
an end, and the Ghanaian military government declared its opposition to the political repression of which it accused Kwame Nkrumah. Both outlawed existing political parties, those of Nigeria's
multiparty system as well as the single party of Ghana. However,
both promised not only to restore civil government as soon as this
could safely be done in their judgment, but also to promote the
resumption of politics and the resumption of its growth. They
planned to do this by different means: in Nigeria at first by reducing the excessive federalism which had been introduced, in Professor Friedrich's term, as a "gadget"; later, after the second military
takeover, by threatening to break up the Federation, so that federal
politics would become international politics. In Ghana the military
government promised to return to some kind of separation of
powers. Both regimes set in motion the preparatory work for adopting new constitutions. The important point to note here is that
both military regimes, though they had replaced radically different

forerunners—one with excessive social mobilization, the other with insufficient or at least reduced social mobilization, to use Professor Huntington's terminology—appeared committed to the further development of a more balanced, healthily growing politics in their respective countries.[13]

This raises an interesting question. Why does there seem to be so much agreement between these two African governments which have overthrown regimes that were so radically different, while there was and is so much disagreement among Western interpreters of the old and new regimes of both countries? The plausible answer, in my judgment, is that the outsiders' evaluations of these African political systems reveal a great deal more about the political views, controversies, and problems of the outsiders themselves than about politics in Africa. They may reveal also why outside interpretations of Africa as a developing area have so far generally not been very realistic, at least in the sense that they have only rarely given accurate forecasts of even the most general trends. By this I do not mean to say that either of the two schools of thought discussed here has been wrong all the time or has deliberately distorted realities at any time. On the contrary, one can analyze recent events in Nigeria, Ghana, the Congo, Uganda, and in other countries that have experienced coups or other "mishaps" on the regional, continental, and global levels, with the perspectives of both the repetitionists and the innovationists and benefit from the mutual complement of mirror images.

An explanation of the Nigerian turnover would not be possible without consideration of both the conventional conservatism of the old regime, to which the innovationists would point, and the relative rapidity with which independence came to the unprepared peoples of a non-nation, to which the repetitionists would point. The coup in Ghana cannot be understood without consideration of President Nkrumah's dictatorial tendencies, which the repetitionists would emphasize, and foreign machinations against him or the fall in cocoa prices, which the innovationists would stress. Understanding of events in the Congo requires probing into both the massive non-African interference and into the unpreparedness for self-government of the Congolese. The troubles of Uganda must be explained with reference to both the outlandish federal constitution with which the British left that colony, and the more general knowl-

[13] See my article, "Political Values in Black Africa," in *Festschrift für Gerhard Leibholz* (Tübingen: J. C. B. Mohr, 1966).

edge we have of the workings of plural societies whose components have unequal substantive and procedural preparation and commitments to the new politics. The apparent failures of such "federal" ventures as the Mali Federation, the East African Federation, the Nigerian Federation, the quasi-pseudo-crypto-federalism of the Belgian-designed *Loi fondamental* of the Congo—an understanding of these benefits from examination of the motives of the colonial powers and their actions, which may have been based upon false analogies, as well as the extent to which, and the reasons for which, events truly analogous to earlier attempts at federation-building were involved. And so forth.

However, none of these situations can be adequately explained by an approach that starts out with the expectation of repetition or of innovation in Africa's politics of development because such an approach appears to be tied too closely (though not necessarily consciously) to certain political positions related to the Cold War. For adequate explanations, we need at least one and probably two additional perspectives.

First we need the "inside" views of the Africans themselves, though these do not have to be taken at face value any more than we take the views of other politicians or political philosophers at face value in an age of ideologism and psychologism. There is, however, a special difficulty in getting African interpretations of African events that have a reasonably high theoretical content. The reason is twofold: Africa's lack, until now, of a separate estate, caste, or profession of political philosophers, and the fact that, with few exceptions like Nkrumah and Senghor, few African politicians have had the time or the inclination to write about political problems in a systematic or at least in an intellectually disciplined way. This is one great merit of Professor Mazrui's contribution to this book, for he may well be unique as a political scientist who serves as an African interpreter of African poltics. At the same time, his necessarily Western training in the craft may also lead him to overintellectualize or to overideologize the operationally relevant thought of African politicians, who have impressed many outside observers, including myself, as comparatively unideological and untheoretic.

In addition to such inside views, we probably also need, for adequate explanations of events of African development, critical outside analyses detached from the various positions that are to some degree related to the policies of the Cold War—if we could only get them!

IV – Africa: Area of the Development of Politics

In conclusion, I shall return, within the context of Black Africa, to the three questions which I posed in the Introduction. Does *development* provide a basis for useful classification? What is it that is developing in these areas? How much can one developing area learn from another?

To deal with the last question first, the history of Black Africa in the decade ending in 1966 suggests not only that one developing area can indeed learn from another, but that African political leaders did in fact learn a great deal from their interpretation of the experiences of the other regions that have achieved an awareness of the possibilities of change through politics since the end of World War II. The Africans were the last to achieve this awareness and therefore went about learning their lessons in a particularly self-conscious way. This may account for their seemingly greater eschewal of false analogies between their own and other situations. Consequently, they may have been enabled to learn from the mistakes of others in a genuinely prospective way, unlike the retrospective way in which constitution-builders (among others) often try to prevent the last political catastrophe instead of the next.

African politicians of development seem to have learned one lesson in particular, which is relevant to the first of my questions. This is the lesson of regional interdependence, on whch they based their consensus on the desirability of continental cooperation. None of the other so-called developing areas equals Africa in that its politicians act as much in awareness of co-existing within an area. In other words, in Africa, leaders of the several states more often show evidence that they think of their countries as subsystems of the regional political system. Since it is precisely this awareness that creates political systems out of human conglomerates held together by mere geographical propinquity or ethnic or social homogeneity,[14] this heightened regional self-consciousness of African politicians also points to an answer to my second question: it is above and before all else politics that is developing in Africa. Through politics, as the uniquely and supremely human activity, Africans are developing and expanding their awareness of the desirable and the

[14] See my "The Utility of Systems Theory," in James C. Charlesworth, ed., *Contemporary Political Analysis* (New York: Free Press of Glencoe, Inc., 1967), and my *World Politics: The Global System* (Homewood, Ill.: The Dorsey Press, 1966), ch. 3.

realizable. What has been going on in Africa is therefore not as much repetition or innovation, as it is a revival of the pure classic tradition of Western philosophy, according to which politics is the master science.

Other Spectrum Books of Interest